the
Modern Quilt
workshop

QUARRY

the Modern Quilt
workshop

PATTERNS, TECHNIQUES, AND DESIGNS
FROM THE FUNQUILTS STUDIO

GLOUCESTER MASSACHUSETTS

QUARRY BOOKS

**Weeks Ringle
and Bill Kerr**

First published in the United States of America by:
Quarry Books, an imprint of
Rockport Publishers, Inc.
33 Commercial Street
Gloucester, Massachusetts 01930-5089
Telephone: (978) 282-9590
Fax: (978) 283-2742
www.rockpub.com

Library of Congress Cataloging-in-Publication Data
Kerr, Bill, 1965-
       The modern quilt workshop : patterns, techniques, and designs from the FunQuilts
Studio / Bill Kerr.
              p.   cm.
       ISBN 1-59253-152-0 (pbk.)
       1. Patchwork—Patterns. 2. Quilting—Patterns. I. Title.
       TT835.K465 2005
       746.46'041—dc22   2004025591

ISBN 1-59253-152-0

10 9 8 7 6 5 4 3 2 1

Design: Bill Kerr

Cover Image: Allan Penn Photography

Printed in Singapore

The authors have made every attempt to verify
measurements, but if you should find any
corrections, they would be glad to be notified.

Contents

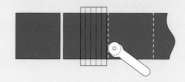

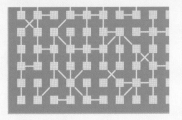

Introduction

Watching someone make a quilt is truly inspiring. Whether it is their first quilt or their twentieth, the process of watching our students select fabric, cut it into pieces, compose a design, and sew it together never fails to cheer us. There is an excitement in their eyes and voices as they describe the satisfaction they get from making something. "I can't believe I made this" are words we frequently hear but never, ever tire of. Inspiring creativity in others is one of the best parts of our work, and it is why we decided to write this book. We want you to challenge yourself, realize your creative potential, and share our great affection for making quilts. We also want you not just to replicate the patterns and colors shown in the samples but also to adapt the patterns to your own color sensibilities and ideas.

When we started teaching, we thought that people would come to our classes to learn how to make quilts. Over the years we have come to understand that the finished quilt is just the tangible evidence of a larger, and arguably more important, experience: that of creating. When students come to us saying that they want to make a quilt, what we usually see are people who want a creative experience and an opportunity for self-expression in the form of a quilt. Ready-made quilts cost a fraction of those made by hobby quiltmakers, yet quiltmakers continue to spend time, money, and energy making quilts because the process of making them is gratifying and fun. For some, it is even healing. Harried mothers of young children, exhausted caregivers of ill parents, and men seeking a creative outlet often find that the process of making something soft and warm is more restorative than anything sold at a drugstore.

With this in mind, we wanted to write a book for quiltmakers that focuses on the process of making a quilt. We want to encourage you to grow as a quiltmaker by gaining new technical skills as well as new insights into the design process. So rather than just offering a series of innovative patterns, we designed a collection of quilts that offers opportunities for improving specific design and technical skills, whether you are a novice or an experienced quiltmaker.

Each of the fifteen quilts in this book has been made in one palette of fabrics and is accompanied by a series of illustrations that shows what the quilt would look like in other colors. Rather than try to make the exact quilt shown, why not think about the colors you find soothing or cheery? What colors put a smile on your face, are meaningful to you, or evoke rich memories? Our goal here is to show you an example and give yourself enough guidance so you can make the perfect quilt for yourself or a loved one. We have also included a section to illustrate techniques we have developed for improving craftsmanship and durability.

Each of us can make only so many quilts in our lifetime. So take your time, enjoy every step of the process, and make it your own.

Appr

How to Use This Book

Some people come to us with a yard of a large-scale print fabric that they love but don't know how to use, whereas others are ready to conquer their fear of piecing curves and circles. Still others have a more general desire to improve their craftsmanship. Some are having their first baby and just want to make a simple baby quilt. We have organized this book to help you find a project that is appropriate to your needs, time, and skill level.

The first section in the book, "Approach and Inspiration," describes our design philosophy and our approach to making quilts. At the end of the first section is an inspirational gallery of photographs that demonstrates interesting color combinations, textures, and patterns that have inspired us.

The second section of the book, "Patterns," features patterns for fifteen quilts. Each pattern lists the technical skills and design principles you will learn by making the quilt. In addition, it also notes the skill level needed to make the quilt and the yardage required for various sizes. Each project also includes color variations of the design so you can see how your color decisions might affect the overall look of the quilt.

Construction techniques unique to each quilt are shown, but more general construction techniques applicable to all the quilts are included in the "Creating the Quilt" section, which follows the "Pattern" section.

"Creating the Quilt," the third section of the book, is divided into two parts. One part guides you through the design of the quilt, while the other teaches general construction, assembly, and finishing techniques useful for making any type of quilt. Templates for each of the fifteen quilts can be found in the appendix along with a list of resources for quiltmakers throughout the world.

Math whizzes may note that there are discrepancies between English and metric conversions. For example, when discussing seam allowances, $\frac{1}{4}$" is not exactly 0.5 cm. Rather than use straight mathematical conversions, we have used measurements in accordance with general sewing conventions found in countries that use the metric system. In other places, it has been necessary to adjust the final size of each quilt because of this difference in seam allowances. In other words, straight mathematical conversions were not always appropriate.

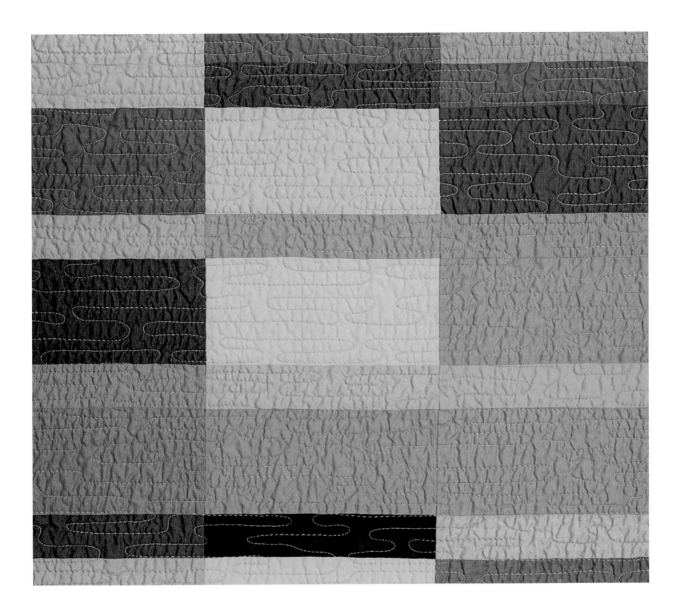

Our Approach to Quiltmaking

We are Modernists. Although we appreciate and admire the quilts of the nineteenth century, our primary interest is in making quilts that are expressive of the time and culture in which we live. We want to contribute new designs and innovative techniques to the quilt world. We want to champion excellent craftsmanship and thoughtful design. With this in mind, we have designed this collection of quilts to offer quiltmakers the chance to try something new. Our goal is to help you make enduring, beautiful quilts, not necessarily those that are quick and easy to assemble.

Through our art and design educations, we have developed a love of color theory, and we never tire of playing with color and seeing the effect that different color combinations have on the design of a quilt. We do not consult color-marketing groups or strive to produce quilts made of this year's "hot" colors; rather, we choose colors that reinforce a larger design intention and are timeless.

Because the focus of our business is the design and making of quilts, we are constantly developing new techniques and designs to keep ourselves fresh and our designs interesting to collectors. Our desire to show you many possi-bilities of a particular pattern is in part our excitement about how different a quilt can look with a few changes, but also a reaction to what we hear from shop owners, editors of quilting magazines, and our own students. Many people have difficulty visualizing how a quilt will look in different colors or at a different scale. We hope that by seeing the various possibilities of a given design you will develop the ability to visualize other patterns in different colors or variations.

We met and married after we each had already acquired design training and opinions about how things could be done. During the ten years in which we have been collaborating, we have influenced each other a great deal. At the same time, we maintain very different working styles and preferences. In the "Creating the Quilt" section, we will provide different opinions about everything from color selection to such burning questions as whether you should put anti-slip feet on your ruler. (Weeks: Absolutely; Bill: No way, they drive me crazy). Our intent is not to confuse you but rather to acknowledge that working styles vary greatly from person to person. We'll give you options. See what works for you.

We're Often Asked…

How much does craftsmanship matter?

Every quilter has seen them or heard about them. They strike fear into the hearts of quilt show aspirants. "They" are a particular species of quilt show judges who have strict notions about how a quilt should be made. One student confessed that she ripped out all the quilting of her queen-size quilt because a judge didn't like it. This story really dismays us. But then again, we don't aspire to those sorts of quilt shows, whereas this student, like many, receives a great deal of gratification from participating in quilt shows and winning prizes.

As we see it, good craftsmanship is not about setting inflexible rules. It is about encouraging people to do the best work they can do because they, not we, will reap the rewards from a job well done. We encourage you to take your time cutting, pin carefully when necessary, and align seams—the quilt is going to be around for a long time, and you want to feel a sense of accomplishment each time you look at it. When deciding how important craftsmanship is, think about how you are going to feel about the craftsmanship in five years. If you aspire to quilt shows, then you need to abide by their standards. But as far as we're concerned, taking your time to make a quilt that is pleasing to you is all that matters.

There are, however, a few things to keep in mind. A quilt with good craftsmanship is a lot easier and more fun to construct than one for which you have to battle every seam. Poor craftsmanship tends to result in more and more problems at every stage of the quilt's construction, which can be very stressful and disappointing to the maker. Don't rush through making a quilt. It will be more stress than it's worth. Conversely, we have seen the unmistakable pride that comes from a student taking the time to cut and piece a curve perfectly or piecing together a complex block with precision. Slow down, take your time, be willing to try a new technique, and reap the rewards of good craftsmanship. Remember, it's supposed to be fun.

Having said that, we know a few people who just do not have the fine motor skills, the desire, or the patience to construct their quilts with care. If you are one of those people, focus on what you do well (color work, or design, or composition) and let the rest go. Piecing improvisationally (see Unfinished Business, page 74) is often a wonderful outlet for those quiltmakers who feel that life is too short to match points. Remember also that, in the end, it's your quilt, and all that matters is that you like it and that you had fun making it.

Why does that circle go off the edge of the quilt?

Look at the photograph on the front page of today's newspaper or flip through your favorite book of paintings. Note that elements in the photograph or painting extend beyond the edge of the piece in most instances. This concept, called "engaging the edge," suggests that the interesting elements extend beyond what the viewer can see. Engaging the edge creates images that often are more dynamic than those in which everything is crowded into the center. Think of the difference in dynamism between that photo on the front page and most posed school photos in which the child sits in isolation.

In the same way, engaging the edge of a quilt can make it seem more dynamic and more interesting to the viewer. Having elements floating on a field of color sometimes works, but some designs are made more dynamic by having an important element in the quilt appear to disappear beyond the edge of the binding. There are no hard and fast rules about engaging the edge, but it is a valuable design concept to understand. Look how the circles of our Eclipse quilt, above, engage the edge.

Where have all the borders gone?

Many of our new students express confusion over why there are no borders on our quilts and why our designs seem to disappear into the binding. In the classes they have taken prior to working with us, they have been told that the border is an essential part of every quilt.

In our art and design training, we learned to look at different types of two-dimensional art to get clues about how to handle the edges of a composition. Many designs become static when surrounded by borders. Sometimes people use borders as fillers because they get tired of making the quilt before it is the size they intended. They figure they will just throw on a border and call it a day. If you find yourself in this position, put the quilt away until you have the energy to finish it properly. It is not worth watering down a beautiful, complex design just because you are tired. It will still be there when you have regained your energy.

Our approach is to determine whether or not the border adds additional interest to the piece. Sometimes a design might need a bit of breathing room, but most of the time, the better solution is to extend the blocks all the way to the edge or add more of the field fabric to the edges. Before you add a border, question whether you really need it. If it's a beautiful quilt already, it will be better without any other element to distract from it. If you're disappointed with it for some reason, finish it, donate it to a charity, and call it a learning experience. A border will not improve it—it will look only like a disappoint-

ing quilt with a border on it. We have all had our quilts that we look at and ponder, "What was I thinking?" Give it away and move on.

Do I need an expensive sewing machine to make a good quilt?

Although there is no doubt that a high-quality sewing machine makes the process of making a quilt easier, the lack of a good sewing machine should not be a deterrent for anyone. Working with an old or unpredictable machine will mean that you have to work more carefully and accept its limitations. In a pinch, remember that some quilt shops or dealers rent machines. You can find tremendous bargains for used machines on the Internet or on trade-ins at dealers. If you buy a reputable brand (ask the staff at a quilt shop which brands are the best for making quilts), a good shop can clean and repair most problems with used machines as well. If you are in the market for a sewing machine, please refer to "The Sewing Machine" in the "Creating the Quilt" section (see page 84).

Inspiration

The most frequent question we are asked is "How do you come up with ideas for quilts?" A close second is "How did you come up with this color combination?" We find that inspiration comes at unexpected times and in unexpected places. You don't need to travel far to find inspiration—you just need to train your eyes to see it. Sometimes it's easier to find inspiration in new places because you notice things that are new more easily than you notice things that are familiar. Whether you spend your day sitting at a desk, milking cows, or changing diapers, here are some things to look for:

Interesting textures: Pay attention to textures on the sidewalk, footprints in mud, the smoothness of hand lotion, the prickle of a fresh pineapple, or the rustic quality of an old brick building. Noticing textures may inspire you to develop a new quilting pattern for your quilt.

Unexpected color combinations: The grocery store is a great place to notice colors. Look at fresh beets next to green grapes, celery next to oranges, watermelons next to Granny Smith apples, Portobello mushrooms next to Spanish onions. Gardening magazines, urban murals, stained-glass windows, and even your spice rack can show you new ways to think about combining colors. If you are stuck on which colors to choose for a quilt, think of an adjective that you would use to describe the quilt you want to make. Then think about the colors you would use to imply that adjective.

Playing with proportion and scale: Look for really big things next to small things, such as this child riding through the grove of trees. Note how the yellow coat, tiny in the overall scale of the picture, transforms the picture. Colors in a quilt need not be used in equal amounts. Be on the lookout for small splashes of color in daily life and the ways in which they can transform an ordinary street scene.

Captivating patterns: Think about the patterns of individual objects, as well as how they look against various backgrounds. For example, the striped car looks even more playful when it is next to a white van; the busy African market looks even busier when everyone is wearing numerous colorful patterns. Try to notice patterns in clothing, tile work, jewelry, and rugs. Combining lots of fabric patterns can be cheerful but can also overwhelm the design of the quilt.

Patterns

Outside the Box

Skill level: simple ├──①──┼──┼──┤ advanced
Technical skills developed: piecing in sequence, aligning points
Design skills developed: exploring color, discerning values, composition
Size shown in photo: full/queen bed quilt

We love designs that have depth and visual dimension. Outside the Box is a play on the traditional checkerboard quilt block. Although the quilt is pieced in blocks, each block appears to have a frame overlapping a square. The pattern is simple to follow, and the large pieces make it a snap even for a bed-sized quilt. The forgiving design makes fabric selection easy as well. Go for analogous colors for the squares and frames and a much darker or lighter background color that won't show seams. The modern, graphic quality of the design combined with its easy construction make this the perfect pattern for a "'tween" or teenager's bedroom. Perhaps it could be a nice learn-to-sew project for a parent, grandparent, uncle, or aunt to take on with the assistance of the recipient.

finished size		wall	napping	twin	full/queen
size	in (w x h)	45 x 45	50 x 72	64 x 87	97 x 100
	cm	125 x 125	139 x 191	160 x 235	237 x 275
blocks	w x h	3 x 3	2 x 4	3 x 5	5 x 6
FABRIC					
box	fabrics total				
	yards	¼	¼	¾	1 ¾
	meters	¼	¼	¾	1 ½
frame	fabrics total				
	yards	½	½	1	2 ¼
	meters	½	½	1	2
background	yards	1 ¾	2 ¾	4	6 ½
	meters	1 ½	2 ½	3 ½	6
backing	yards	1 ½	3 ½	5 ½	8
	meters	1 ½	3 ½	5	7 ½
binding	yards	½	¾	1	1
	meters	½	¾	1	1

The Modern Quilt Workshop

Variations

Having made this quilt in a wide range of palettes, we've discovered how versatile the pattern is. As long as the squares and frames read clearly, you can select any palette. When made with soft, analogous blues and greens, it becomes a calm quilt, reminiscent of a spa. Executed with a rainbow of colors, it is youthful. Using just three colors creates a strong graphic statement that could make your bed the centerpiece of the room.

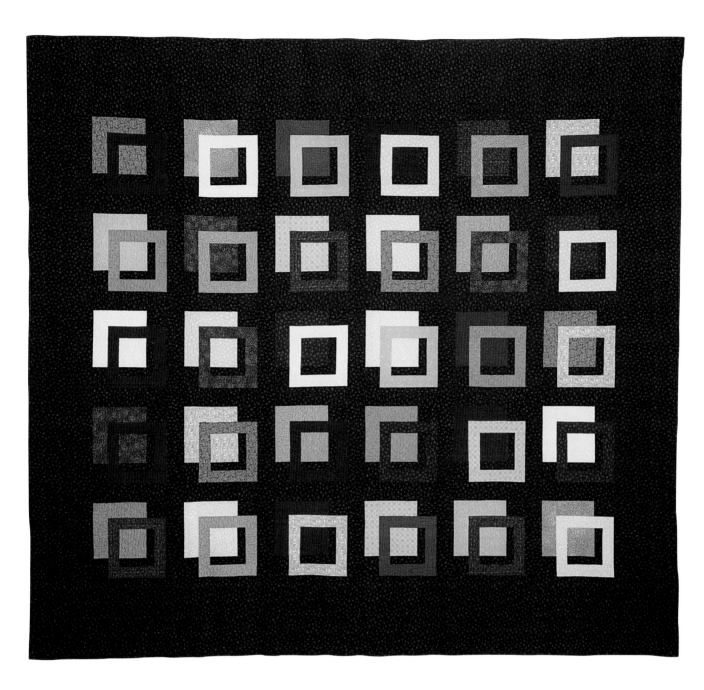

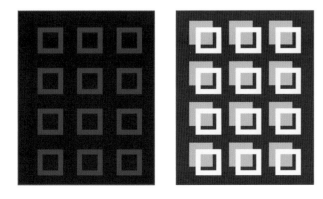

PIECES	wall	napping	twin	full/queen
background column strips	2 ea. 3¼"x40" (9 x 109 cm)	3 ea. 3¼"x26" (9 x 70 cm)	4 ea. 3¼"x40" (9 x 110 cm)	5 ea. 3¼"x68" (9 x 186 cm)
2 sides	3¼" x 40" (9 x 109 cm)	9" x 26" (23 x 70 cm)	10" x 40" (25 x 110 cm)	10" x 68" (25 x 186 cm)
top & bottom strips	3¼" x 45" (9 x 125 cm)	14" x 72" (35.5 x 192 cm)	14" x 87" (35.5 x 236 cm)	14" x 100" (35.5 x 276 cm)
number per block (total)				
4¾" x 4¾" **A** (12 x 12 cm)	1 (9)	1 (8)	1 (15)	1 (30)
1¾" x 4¾" **B** (4.5 x 12 cm)	1 (9)	1 (8)	1 (15)	1 (30)
1¾" x 6" **C** (4.5 x 15.5 cm)	1 (9)	1 (8)	1 (15)	1 (30)
2¼" x 6" **D** (5.5 x 15.5 cm)	2 (18)	2 (16)	2 (30)	2 (60)
2¼" x 9½" **E** (5.5 x 24.5 cm)	2 (18)	2 (16)	2 (30)	2 (60)
2¾" x 6½" **F** (7 x 16.5 cm)	1 (9)	1 (8)	1 (15)	1 (30)
2¾" x 3½" **G** (7 x 9 cm)	2 (18)	2 (16)	2 (30)	2 (60)
2¾" x 8¾" **H** (7 x 22.5 cm)	1 (9)	1 (8)	1 (15)	1 (30)
3¼" x 11¾" **I** (9 x 30.5 cm)	6 total	4 total	10 total	24 total

Directions

When we make this quilt, we always do the cutting first, then assemble the quilt block-by-block. When piecing, you can use our leapfrog method introduced on page 91 for efficiency.

1. Cut pieces **A** to **I** according to the cutting chart and sort the pieces into piles by fabric and shape.

2. Lay out the pieces needed for one block. (*Figure 1*)

3. For efficiency in piecing and ironing, chain-piece **A** to **B**, **C** to **D**, **F** to **G**, and another **G** to **H**, then iron the seams open. Continue piecing in the sequence diagrammed (*Figure 2*) to make the finished block.

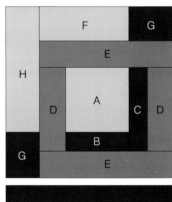

figure 1

Design Tips

When selecting fabric, divide the fabrics for the frames and squares into two piles: the lighter ones and the darker ones. Note in the sample shown that the frame is sometimes the darker fabric and sometimes the lighter fabric, but that it always contrasts with the fabric used in the square. Choose pairs of fabrics that contrast with each other so the frames won't appear to be blending into the squares and vice versa. The fabric you choose for the background should also contrast nicely with those used for the frames and squares.

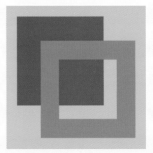

Good contrast

Insufficient contrast of value between frame and background

4. Repeat steps 1 through 3 to make the number of blocks required. Vary the fabrics for the frames and squares for variety.

5. Lay out the blocks to ensure that the most-attention-getting blocks are evenly distributed. Number the blocks to record the layout.

6. Piece in vertical rows, piecing background row strips **I** between each block. (*Figure 3*)

7. Join the vertical rows, piecing background column strips between rows.

8. Add the top, bottom, and side background strips.

9. Layer the top, batting, and backing, then quilt and bind. For more information on quilting and binding, see "Making the Quilt" on page 84.

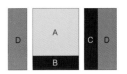

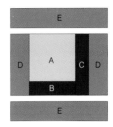

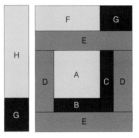

figure 2

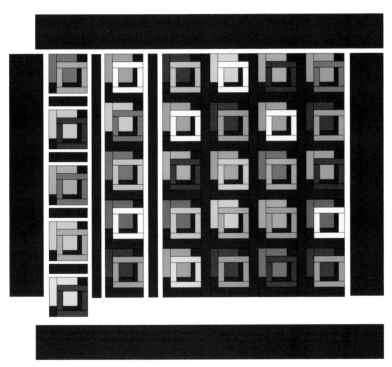

figure 3

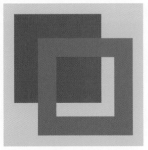

Needs more contrast of hue between square and frame

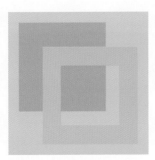

Frame and square have insufficient contrast of value

Plain Spoken

Skill level: simple ├──①──┼───┼───┤ advanced
Technical skills developed: aligning points, precision cutting
Design skills developed: working with color subtleties, composition
Size shown in photo: napping quilt

Solid fabrics are the underdogs of the fabric world. They sit alone in forgotten corners of quilt shops, losing out in the competition for your attention to shelves of flamboyant prints and trendy batiks. We designed Plain Spoken as a reminder of the power and beauty of solids. The basic building block of this quilt couldn't be simpler—one wide rectangle sewn to a narrower rectangle.

At first glance, the napping quilt shown appears to contain just a handful of different fabrics. Look closely—it has more than two dozen. We could make this quilt in different color palettes over and over and never tire of it. Power to the underdog!

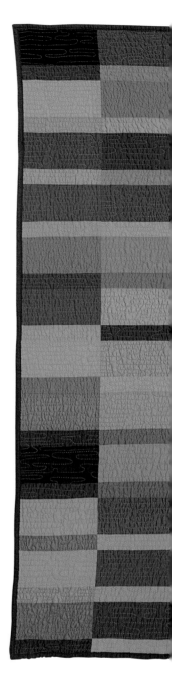

finished size		wall	napping	twin	full/queen
size	*in (w x h)*	38 x 42	51 x 77	63 x 91	85 x 97
	cm	103 x 108	138 x 198	172 x 234	230 x 252
blocks	*w x h*	9 x 6	12 x 11	15 x 13	20 x 14
FABRIC					
front	*yards*	2	3 ½	5 ½	8
	meters	2	3 ½	5	7 ½
backing	*yards*	1 ¼	3 ½	5 ½	8
	meters	1 ¼	3 ½	5	7 ½
binding	*yards*	½	¾	1	1
	meters	½	¾	1	1

Variations

This quilt sparkles in all its incarnations. Soothing pastels are far from predictable in this contemporary pattern. When reduced to pale yellow, orange, and red analogous colors, the quilt whispers softness. Turning up the volume on saturation can bring a bold twist with fuchsias, pinks, and purples popping to life. A napping quilt in desert colors would bring a hint of color to a neutral living room. Finally, look how a few reds tossed in among blacks and grays create a peppery accent.

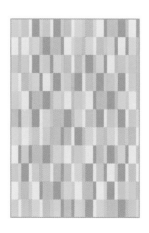
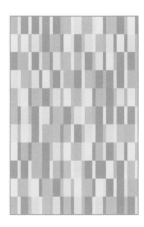

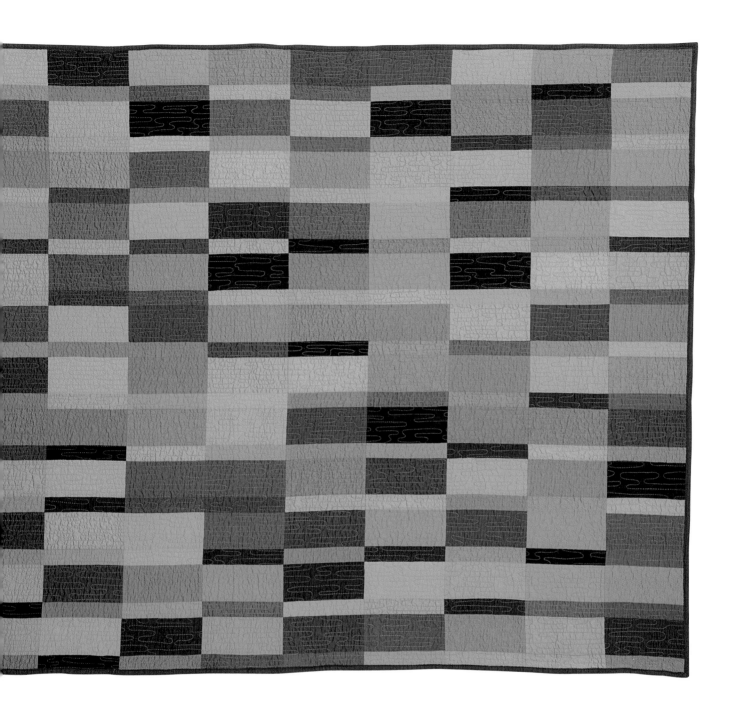

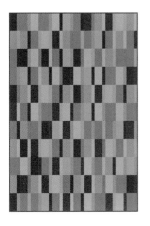
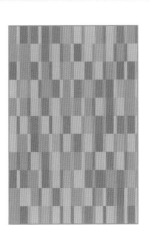
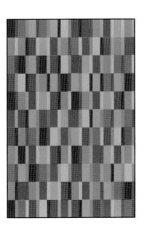

PIECES	wall	napping	twin	full/queen
3 ½" x 7 ½" rectangles (9 x 19 cm)	54	132	195	280
1 ¾" x 7 ½" rectangles (4.5 x 19 cm)	54	132	195	280

Directions

1. Cut the wide and narrow rectangles as specified in the cutting chart.

2. Randomly piece together narrow and wide rectangles of different fabrics into pairs. (*Figure 1*). This is the basic block of the quilt. You can chain-piece one pair after another for efficiency. Learn more about chain piecing on page 90 of the "Making the Quilt" section.

3. Iron open the seams.

4. If the size of quilt you are making has an odd number of blocks in each row, set aside one block per row to terminate it.

5. Randomly pair the remaining blocks and sew them together. (*Figure 2*)

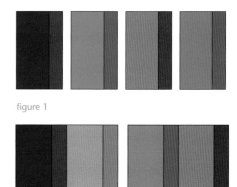

figure 1

figure 2

Design Tips

Many manufacturers produce a wide range of solids, but most quilt shops carry only a limited selection. To get the most subtleties, purchase solids from various manufacturers. One company's pale pink will be slightly brighter than another's, or their forest green may be a bit more olive than that from another company. There may also be a difference within the same mill from bolt to bolt if they were dyed in different batches. The palettes illustrated show the richness you can achieve when you add colors to bridge the hues and values of a basic palette. Though each change is subtle, the final palette is distinctly richer than the initial one.

6. Lay out the quilt row by row. Whereas the earlier pairings were random, you now should pay attention to composition, moving pieces around if you have awkward adjacencies or similar fabrics touching. Be on the lookout for distracting patterns or repetitions of colors that develop. If the size of quilt you are making has an odd number of pairs in each row, use the pairs you set aside in step 4 to terminate each row. (*Figure 3*)

7. Piece together the rows. You can use the leapfrogging technique described on pages 91–92. Iron open the seams.

8. Piece the rows to each other and iron open the seams. To align the rows precisely, pin through the seams of the rows. (*Figure 4*)

9. Layer the top, batting, and backing, then quilt and bind. For more information on quilting and binding, see "Making the Quilt" on page 84.

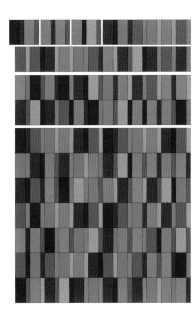

figure 3

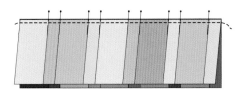

figure 4

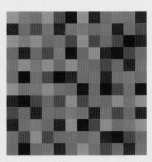

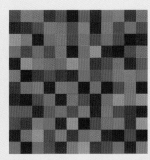

A palette of seven colors   *Two colors added*   *Two more colors added*   *Yet two more colors added*

Redwork

Skill level: simple ⊢—①—+—+—⊣ advanced
Technical skills developed: machine quilting
Design skills developed: composition
Size shown in photo: wall hanging

Redwork refers to a style of embroidery that was popular between 1880 and 1940. Traditionally, designs were printed on small squares of muslin and sold by dry goods merchants. Ladies and children would buy squares, embroider them with red embroidery floss, and incorporate them into their quilts. The process used to color the floss was developed in Turkey, and the shade of red often used in these pieces is known as Turkey Red. We wanted to design a quilt that was all about the quilting and honored this simple yet charming technique. Rather than embroider designs and then quilt them, we use the quilting to serve both the decorative role of embroidery and the functional role of quilting. Making the quilt reversible also adds a new twist to the tradition. This style of quilting and embroidery was also done using indigo blue floss, but in our minds, this simple design lends itself to any combination of contrasting thread and fabric.

finished size		wall	napping	twin	full/queen
size	*in (w x h)*	28 x 38	48 x 72	62 x 90	80 x 90
	cm	72 x 96	122 x 182	160 x 230	205 x 230
FABRIC					
front	*yards*	1	3	5 ½	6
	meters	1	3	5	5 ½
back	*yards*	1 ½	3	5 ½	6
	meters	1 ½	3	5	5 ½
binding	*yards*	½	¾	1	1
	meters	½	¾	1	1

Variations

Though this quilt began as an homage to the redwork of our quiltmaking ancestors, color variations are fun to explore. Color combinations that work well must have sufficient contrast between the thread and the fabric. By having the background stitching match the background, you could quilt the circles in contrasting colors.

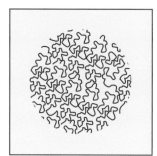

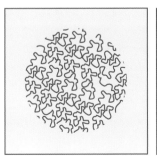
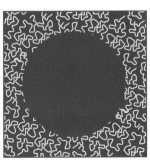
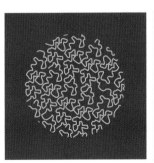

Reverse side

PIECES	wall	napping	twin	full/queen
front	30" x 40"	50" x 74"	64" x 92"	82" x 92"
	(76 x 101 cm)	(127 x 187 cm)	(162 x 234 cm)	(208 x 234 cm)
back	30" x 40"	50" x 74"	64" x 92"	82" x 92"
	(76 x 101 cm)	(127 x 187 cm)	(162 x 234 cm)	(208 x 234 cm)

Design Tips

The success of this quilt lies in the way the quilting defines the edges of the circles. If your stitching is too big, the edges of the circles will not be clear. Rather than look like crisp, graphic circles, they will just look like white blobs. So, before you embark on this quilt, make some samples to gain a sense of how far apart the stitches have to be to get the circles to read. We generally stitch lines about $1/4$" (0.6 cm) to $1/2$" (1.2 cm) apart, which takes longer but gives the quilt a wonderful texture and makes the circles very apparent. These illustrations show what a difference dense quilting provides. Make sure that you use color-fast thread and remember that the thread will always look darker in the quilt once it is washed and dried. Audition a couple of different reds by placing a single strand on the white fabric. Good cotton quilting thread is thicker than polyester thread and will show up more boldly in the quilting.

Directions

1. Select and cut two fabrics for your two sides, piecing if necessary to achieve the dimension shown in the chart. Iron the pieces flat.

2. Gather a collection of at least eight pots, pans, bowls, and other circular household objects ranging from 4" to 12" (10–30 cm) in diameter. Spread out one side of your quilt on the floor. Using schoolboard chalk or a washable chalk pencil, trace a series of circles onto the fabric. Start at one end of the quilt, chalking a big circle first, then surrounding it with circles of other sizes. Leave some space between circles. This process doesn't have to be precise. (*Figure 1*)

3. Continue chalking until the entire quilt is covered in circles. (*Figure 2*)

4. Layer the chalked top, batting, and backing. Baste together, following the directions in the "Making the Quilt" section on page 84.

5. Because this quilt is about the quilting, the choice of thread color is important. We quilted the circles with thread that matched the white background fabric and quilted the area around the circles with red to give our quilt a lacy look. Because we used the same thread on top and in the bobbin, the back is a reverse image of the front.

6. Quilt the interior of the circles, keeping the quilting as dense as you can manage. We used a spiral stitch for the sample. You should choose a stitch that is manageable for you to do densely and consistently. A simple stipple works fine, too. Quilt all the way up to the chalked line but not over it. Take care that your stitching reinforces the form of the circle.

7. When you have quilted all of the circles, change your thread to the color you have chosen for the background and begin quilting. We used a stipple stitch because it is easy to maneuver through the awkward spaces between circles. Use any stitch that you can quilt densely and control well.

8. Finish quilting the background and bind. For more information on quilting and binding, see "Making the Quilt" on page 84.

figure 1

figure 2

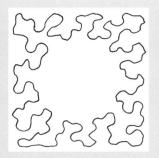

Once Upon a Time

Skill level: simple ├──②──┼──┼──┤ advanced

Technical skills developed: precision cutting, aligning points, strip piecing

Design skills developed: color selection, improvisational composition

Size shown in photo: napping quilt

Once Upon a Time is a storytelling quilt for parents and their children. Let your child pick a starting square, then follow the line to a connected square and start creating a story. There are hundreds of paths you can follow and unlimited stories you can tell. Here's an example starting at the lower-left corner of the quilt:

"Once upon a time, there was a blue elephant named Ellie and a purple monkey named Mimi who went looking for their friend, Sally Spider. Sally was tired from weaving her web all day and said, 'Let's go to the beach!' Grabbing their sunglasses, Ellie, Mimi, and Sally skipped all the way to the ocean. As they were swimming in the waves, they heard a big splash and saw their friend, Freddy the Frog... ."

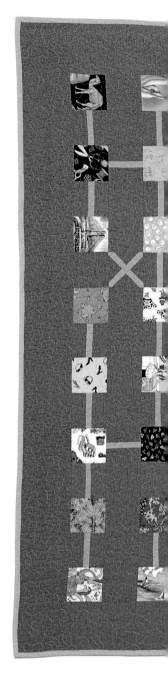

finished size		wall	napping	twin	full/queen
size	*in (w x h)*	40 x 40	51 x 75	69 x 93	88 x 99
	cm	105 x 105	135 x 195	185 x 250	220 x 260
blocks	*w x h*	11 x 11	15 x 23	21 x 29	25 x 29
FABRIC					
background	*yards*	1¼	3	4¾	6½
	meters	1¼	3	4¾	6
story line	*yards*	¼	½	¾	1
	meters	¼	½	¾	1
story squares		36	96	165	195
backing	*yards*	1¼	3½	5½	8
	meters	1¼	3½	5	7½
binding	*yards*	½	¾	1	1
	meters	½	¾	1	1

Variations

Use color combinations that offer ample contrast between the field fabric and the story lines. The color wheel shows the nearly complementary relationship of the blue and yellow colors in the original palette.

The variations shown at right use colors that have contrast of hue (pink/yellow) or contrast of value (light/dark).

Avoid using colors of similar hue and value. For instance, a medium blue line on a medium green field would be hard to see.

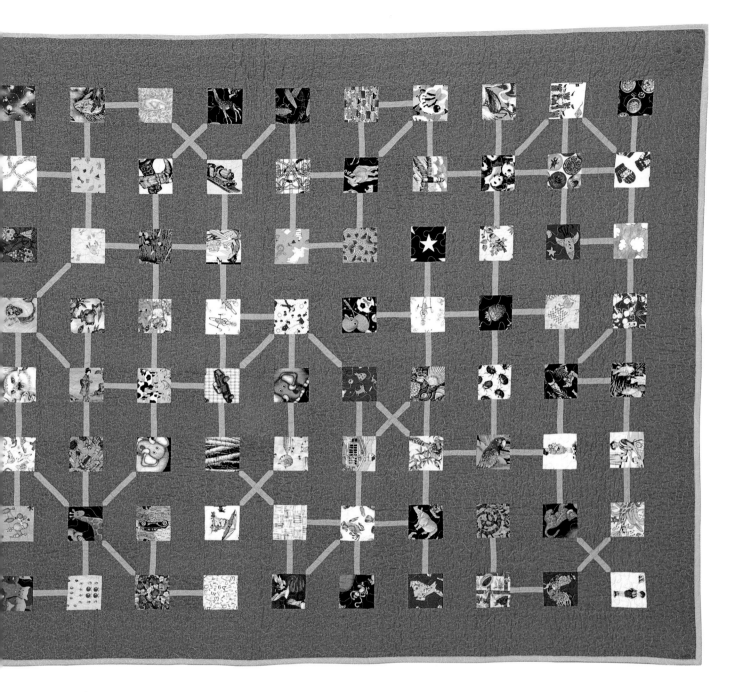

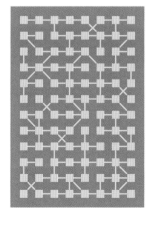

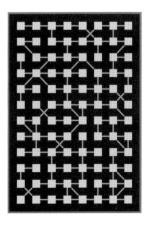
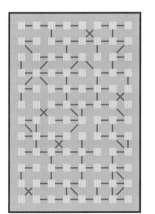

BLOCKS	wall	napping	twin	full/queen
story	36	96	165	195
straight story line	27	85	150	178
background	50	141	244	294
diagonal story line	5	18	35	42
crossed story line	3	5	15	16
Strips				
1" x 40" storylines (2.5 x 100 cm)	5	11	21	24
2 ends	3" x 34" (8 x 90 cm)	3" x 46" (8 x 120 cm)	3" x 65" (8 x 170 cm)	6" x 75" (15 x 195 cm)
2 sides	3" x 40" (8 x 110 cm)	3" x 77" (8 x 200 cm)	3" x 95" (8 x 250 cm)	6" x 100" (15 x 265 cm)

Directions

This quilt is a grid composed of three basic blocks: story squares, field squares, and story line squares. The story line squares can have horizontal, vertical, diagonal, or crossed story lines. Refer to the quilt information chart for the number of blocks needed for each quilt size.

1. Cut novelty fabrics into 3 1/2" (9 cm) squares.

2. Cut 3 1/2" x 40" (9 x 102 cm) strips of the background fabric. Trim these into 3 1/2" (9 cm) squares. Each strip yields 11 blocks. (*Figure 1*)

3. To make the straight story line blocks, cut two background strips 1 3/4" x 40" (4.5 x 102 cm) and one story line strip 1" x 40" (2.5 x 102 cm). Sew these together. (*Figure 2*)

4. Iron open the seams and cut into 3 1/2" (9 cm) square blocks. (*Figure 3*). Each strip yields 11 story line blocks.

5. To make diagonal story line blocks, cut plain blocks from step 2 in half from corner to corner. (*Figure 4*)

6. Sew the resulting triangles to 1" x 40" (2.5 x 102 cm) story line strips. You should be able to piece 7 triangles to each strip. Chalk a line across the strip from the end points of each triangle. (*Figure 5*)

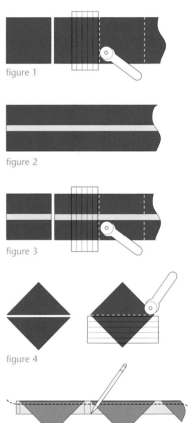

figure 1

figure 2

figure 3

figure 4

figure 5

Design Tips

This is a great chance to use those novelty fabrics you've been collecting, as well as an excuse to find delightful prints of flowers, lightning bugs, umbrellas, frogs, and all your favorite things. As you cut your squares, remember that you will lose the outer 1/4" (0.5 cm) in the seam allowance. These first two photos show how the seam allowance affects the final image.

Only the lion will show

Three animals will show in the final block

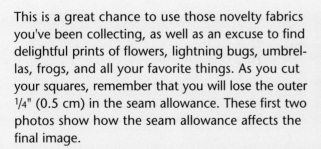

7. Iron open the seams.

8. Align remaining triangles with your marks and sew. (*Figure* 6)

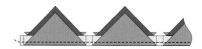

figure 6

9. Iron open the seams and trim into 3 ½" (9 cm) squares. (*Figure* 7)

10. To make crossed story line squares, cut a diagonal story line block in half in the other direction. (*Figure* 8)

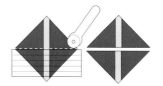

figure 7

11. Align and sew the resulting triangles on a story line strip as you did in steps 6 through 8.

12. Iron open the seams and trim into 3 ½" (9 cm) squares. (*Figure* 9)

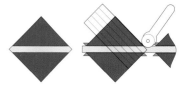

figure 8

13. Laying out this quilt—much like the stories you will tell with it—is improvisational. You don't have to place the story lines exactly as shown in the photo. Rather, lay them out in a way that offers lots of choices (including dead ends, which provide a good way to end a story). When you are happy with the layout, number the pieces with chalk so you can sew them together in the right order.

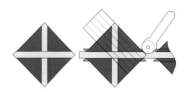

figure 9

14. Assemble the quilt by pinning together rows. For the first row, alternate a story square with either a connector or plain background square. (*Figure* 10)

15. The second row is made of only story line or plain background squares, pinned together in a long chain. Using the leapfrogging technique described on pages 91–92, continue sewing until all rows are formed, then piece the rows together.

16. Cut the background ends and sides. They will be slightly longer than necessary. Attach the top and bottom, then trim flush. Attach the sides and trim flush.

17. Layer top, batting, and backing, then quilt and bind. For more information on quilting and binding, see "Making the Quilt," page 84.

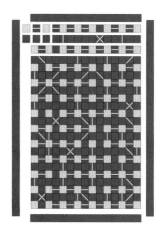

figure 10

To minimize the appearance of the seams, select a small-scale "all-over" or monochromatic print for the field fabric. Avoid large-scale or directional prints. The quilt shown above uses a blue fabric with a subtle black overprint. When the blocks are pieced together and quilted, they read as a single fabric, and the seams virtually disappear.

The pattern betrays the center seam

The pattern disguises the center seam

Marquee

Technical skills developed: strip piecing
Design skills developed: understanding contrast, color proportion
Size shown in photo: queen bed quilt

The flashing lights of marquees in New York's Times Square inspired us to design this quilt. We tried to capture the mesmerizing movement and energy of those lights in the strips of colors that surround the centers of the blocks.

This quilt looks great from a distance and rewards you with detail as you come closer. With its efficient strip piecing and cutting and large blocks, it makes for a manageable bed quilt project. Its forgiving design and construction also make it ideal for a novice.

finished size		wall	napping	twin	full/queen
size	*in (w x h)*	47 x 47	47 x 76	66 x 95	85 x 104
	cm	119 x 119	119 x 193	167 x 241	216 x 264
blocks	w x h	5 x 5	5 x 8	7 x 10	9 x 11
FABRIC					
field	total fabric				
	yards	2	3	5	7
	meters	2	3	4 ½	6 ½
marquee	total fabric				
	yards	2 ¼	4	6	8 ½
	meters	2	3 ¾	5 ½	8
backing	*yards*	1 ½	3 ½	5 ½	9
	meters	1 ½	3 ¼	5	8 ½
binding	*yards*	½	¾	1	1
	meters	½	¾	1	1

Variations

This quilt lends itself to countless color variations, but there must be sufficient contrast between the marquee fabrics and the field fabric.

The following illustrations show two types of contrast: contrast of hue and contrast of value. (There are many other contrasts, such as contrast of saturation, contrast of pattern, contrast of scale, and so on, but we'll concentrate on these two for now.)

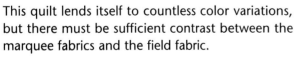

Contrast of hue and value makes the block dynamic

Contrast of value will make the marquee more dominant

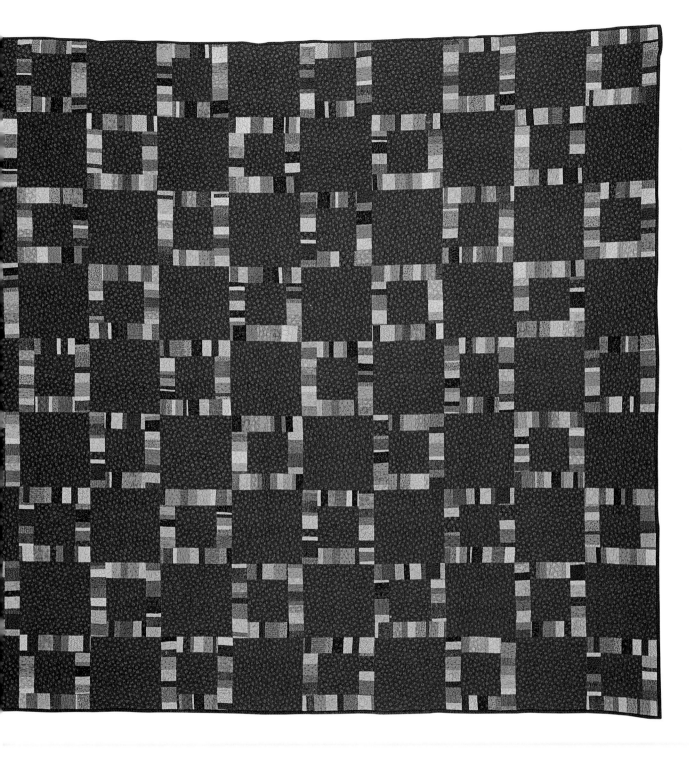

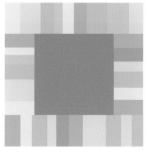

A darker center makes the marquee more luminous

Contrasting hue and value makes the block bolder

Less contrast makes the block subtle

Less contrast makes the block less dynamic

PIECES	wall	napping	twin	full/queen
10" x 10" squares (25 x 25 cm)	12	20	35	50
6" x 6" squares (15 x 15 cm)	13	20	35	49
12" x 40" strip sets (30 x 102 cm)	5	8	14	20

Directions

1. Cut strips of the various marquee fabrics from selvage to selvage. These strips should vary in width from 1" to 2 ½" (2.5–6.5 cm).

2. Mix up the strips and sew them together to make the specified number of sets that are each roughly 12" (30 cm) wide and 42" (105 cm) long. Each set should be different. (*Figure 1*)

3. Cut these striped bands into 2 ½" (6 cm)-wide strips (*Figure 2*)

4. Sew together three of the 2 ½" (6 cm)-wide strips to form a longer strip. Mix up and rotate the strips as you piece them to achieve maximum variety. (*Figure 3*)

5. Chain-piece the center squares to the marquee strips. (*Figure 4*). (For more on chain-piecing, see page 90.)

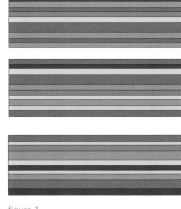

figure 1

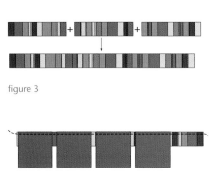

figure 3

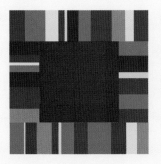

figure 4

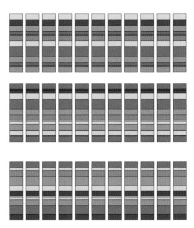

figure 2

Design Tips

Because Marquee is made of many slivers of fabric, it is a great opportunity to play with proportion. These illustrations show the difference between using a few light or bright fabrics as accents and using many so they become dominant and the darks become accents.

6. Iron open the seams and trim flush. (*Figure 5*)

7. Repeat on opposite side. (*Figure 6*)

8. Repeat on top (*Figure 7*) and bottom. (*Figure 8*)

9. Lay out the quilt, alternating pieced squares and background squares. Number the rows with chalk to keep from mixing them up. (*Figure 9*)

10. You can piece more efficiently using the leapfrogging technique described on pages 91–92, sewing until all rows are formed, then piece rows together.

11. Layer the top, batting, and backing, then quilt and bind. For more information on quilting and binding, see "Making the Quilt," beginning on page 84.

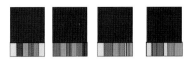

figure 5

figure 6

figure 7

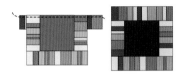

figure 8

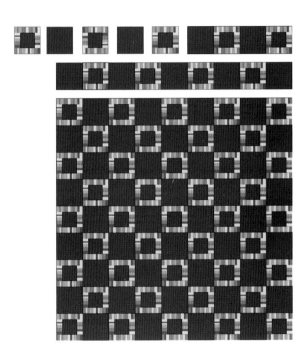

figure 9

Zipper

Technical skills developed: aligning points, chain piecing
Design skills developed: color selection, understanding value
Size shown in photo: napping quilt

In traditional quilt designs, blocks are designed as independent units, usually squares. Our Zipper quilt reflects our fascination with pieces that appear to be interlocking. Although you need to pay attention to the sequencing of pieces and to the layout of the quilt, the cutting and sewing are simple and manageable even for a beginner. Being able to see clearly the "teeth" of the zipper is important, so avoid any large-scale, multicolored florals or stripes. For the binding, we chose a gray that is the same value as the blues and greens but is not seen elsewhere in the quilt, thereby making the edge of the quilt clean. The thread color for the quilting is the same gray, and we selected an elongated quilting stitch so we could quilt each of the teeth individually.

finished size		wall	napping	twin	full/queen
size	*in (w x h)*	40 x 42	46 x 77	64 x 91	88 x 91
	cm	106 x 105	122 x 192	170 x 227	234 x 227
blocks	*w x h*	7 x 6	8 x 11	11 x 13	15 x 13
FABRIC					
front	assorted fabrics total				
	yards	¼ ea. of 9	½ ea. of 8	¾ ea. of 11	¾ ea. of 13
	meters	¼ ea. of 9	½ ea. of 8	½ ea. of 11	½ ea. of 13
backing	*yards*	1 ½	3 ½	5 ½	8
	meters	1 ½	3	5	7 ½
binding	*yards*	½	¾	1	1
	meters	½	¾	1	1

Variations

This design lends itself to analogous color palettes. The warm, earthy red of the first variation contrasts with the cool blues and greens in the sample. The second variation, which uses a warm palette but with much lighter values, makes the quilt quite delicate, with only a suggestion of the zipper form. In the third illustration, there is heightened contrast between light and dark, emphasizing the individual blocks as much as the overall pattern. In the fourth example, we show a multicolored palette that might be appropriate in a Victorian-era home. No matter which palette you choose, remember to avoid fabrics with large-scale patterns or highly contrasting patterns, because they will appear fractured and chaotic when the teeth are sewn to the main body of the block.

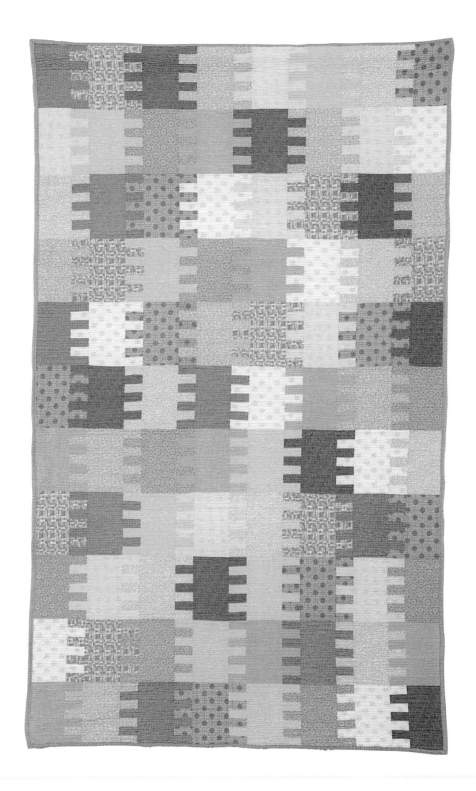

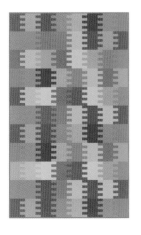   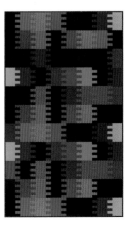

PIECES	wall	napping	twin	full/queen
	pieces of different fabrics			
4 ½" x 7 ½" rectangle **A** (11.5 x 18.5 cm)	4 ea. of 9	12 ea. of 8	15 ea. of 11	15 ea. of 13
2 ½" x 1 ½" rectangle **B** (6.5 x 3.5 cm)	28 ea. of 9	84 ea. of 8	105 ea. of 11	105 ea. of 13

Directions

1. Cut the required number of pieces shown on the cutting chart. For each piece **A** you will have seven of **B**. (*Figure 1*)

2. Sort the pieces of each fabric into **A** pieces and **B** pieces.

3. Select an **A** block for the top corner. To its right, place a different **A** block. Between them, place **B** rectangles which are the teeth of the zipper. Make sure that you select four **B** teeth that match the first **A** block and three **B** teeth that match the second **A** block. (*Figure 2*)

4. Sew the row of teeth together, then iron open the seams (*Figure 3*)

5. Continue laying out the row by alternating blocks and teeth, finishing the row with a plain **A** block.

6. Piece together the **A** blocks with the strips of teeth to form the quilt rows. (*Figure 4*)

7. Lay out, number, and then piece the remaining rows. Avoid placing the same fabrics directly above or below each other.

8. Layer the top, batting, and backing, then quilt and bind. For more information on quilting and binding, see "Making the Quilt," beginning on page 84.

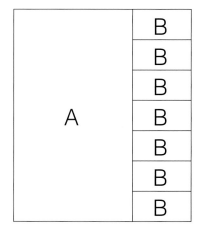

figure 1

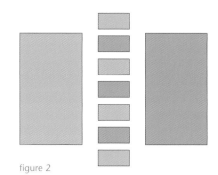

figure 2

Design Tips

In our classes, we introduce a design concept we call "bridging." We use this term to refer to the intervals between hues or values. For example, we have both darks and lights in this quilt, but there isn't a lot of distracting contrast because we have lots of medium-value fabrics to bridge the lights and darks. If you were to assign numbers to the values, with one being the lightest and ten being the darkest, you would want to use fabrics that would have values of everything between one and ten. If you used only fives through eights, including a fabric with a value of one would be distracting. You need to bridge the differences at every interval possible. Similarly, note how the colors range from pale mint green to sapphire blue. We have used some fabrics that contain blues and greens as well.

figure 3

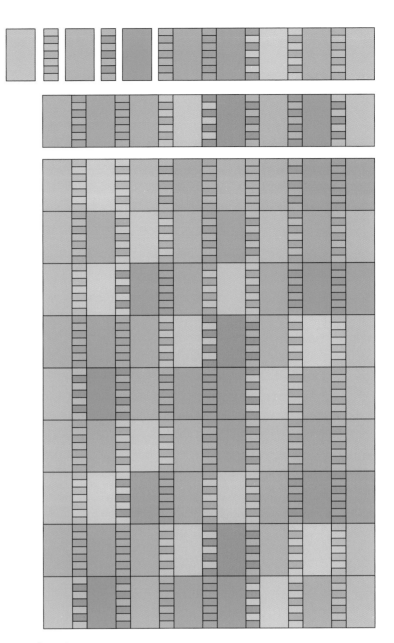

figure 4

This palette has strong
jumps in value

This palette bridges values
smoothly

This palette has strong
jumps in hue and value

This palette bridges hues
and values smoothly

Confetti

Skill level: simple ⊢─┼─②─┼─┤ advanced

Technical skills developed: piecing triangles, piecing in sequence, using templates, making a pieced binding

Design skills developed: color, composition

Size shown in photo: wall hanging (baby quilt)

It happens all the time. Someone who has never made a quilt wants to make a baby quilt for her sister, best friend, or daughter who is due in a month. There is inevitably some constraint such as "and the shower is this Saturday." So here is a contemporary, gender-neutral quilt that can be whipped up quickly. Although pink and baby blue are sweet, remember that this quilt will last for years, so choose fabric that will be appropriate for a preschooler as well. We used batiks because they hide stains, and the large pieces show off the irregular patterns of the fabric nicely. By changing the colors and size, the quilt can just as easily be great for your own bed. Although the pieces are large and easy to assemble, you need to be careful when aligning them. Be diligent about labeling the pieces as you cut them, or you will have a difficult time remembering what goes where.

finished size		wall	napping	twin	full/queen
size	*in (w x h)*	32 x 40	48 x 80	64 x 96	88 x 96
	cm	82 x 102	122 x 204	163 x 244	224 x 244
blocks	*w x h*	4 x 5	6 x 10	8 x 12	11 x 12
FABRIC					
front	assorted fabrics total				
	yards	1 ½	4	6	8 ½
	meters	1 ½	4	5 ½	8
backing	*yards*	1 ¼	3 ½	5 ½	8
	meters	1 ¼	3 ½	5	7 ½
binding	*yards*	½	¾	1	1
	meters	½	¾	1	1

Variations

Like the sample, this first variation is a similar range of hues. However, the much lighter values make it reminiscent of rainbow sherbet, cool and refreshing on a hot summer day. The pale pink, yellow, and orange version relies on an analogous color palette to create a quilt for the family that is sure to dress their baby girl in pink. A range of blues and blue violets makes a more traditional boy's quilt. Selecting deep colors transforms it from a baby quilt to a throw perfect for a paneled study. Bright yellows and reds could perk up any teen's room.

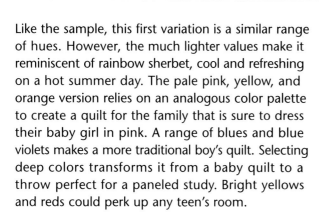

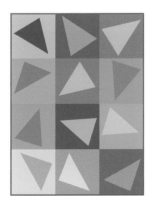

BLOCKS	wall	napping	twin	full/queen
A, A1, A2, A3 each	7	20	32	44
B, B1, B2, B3 each	7	20	32	44
C, C1, C2, C3 each	6	20	32	44

Directions

1. Transfer the templates found in the appendix onto template plastic.

2. Cut the center triangles **A** and pieces **A1**, **A2**, and **A3** that will form the background of the block. You can cut up to four pieces from each template by stacking four pieces of fabric on top of one another and cutting through all at once. Immediately after you cut, however, label each piece with chalk. On the center triangle, label the three sides **A1**, **A2**, and **A3**. On the background pieces, chalk the piece number on the edge shown because it will mate to the corresponding edge of the center triangle. This is especially critical with solids and batiks, which look the same on the front and back. (*Figure 1*)

3. Piece the edge marked **A1** on each **A** center to the edge of the background piece marked **A1**. Iron the seams open. You can use the leapfrogging method described on pages 91–92 for efficiency. (*Figure 2*)

4. To this, piece the edge marked **A2** on the center to the edge of the background piece marked **A2**. Iron the seams open. (*Figure 3*)

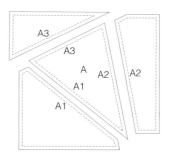

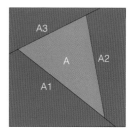

figure 1

figure 3

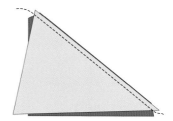

figure 2

Design Tips

Once you have made your blocks, lay them out on a design wall or on the floor and note the direction of the narrowest point of each triangle. Rotate the blocks so they are all pointing in different direction and no awkward patterns have formed. Check also to make sure that the most vibrant blocks are not all in one corner or in one row.

The upper row repeats direction

Three of the corners are too similar

5. To this, piece the edge marked **A3** on the center to the edge of the background piece marked **A3**. Iron the seams open. (*Figure 4*)

6. Repeat steps 2 through 5 for the **B** and **C** blocks. (*Figure 5*)

7. Lay out the blocks and assemble them in rows, ironing open each seam as you go. (*Figure 6*)

8. Piece together the rows and iron open the seams.

9. Layer the top, batting, and backing, then quilt. For more information on quilting, see "Making the Quilt," beginning on page 84.

figure 4

10. To make the pieced binding, cut strips of the colors you want to use in various lengths between 3" and 6" (7.5–15 cm). Chain-piece them together alternating lengths and colors. When you have a pieced strip of binding equal in length to the perimeter of your quilt, follow the instructions for binding on page 103.

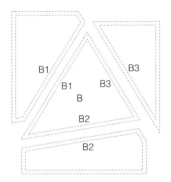

figure 5

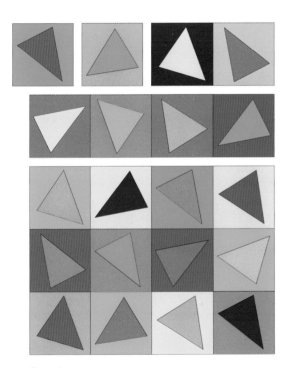

figure 6

The lower corner is overly red

The blocks are more evenly distributed

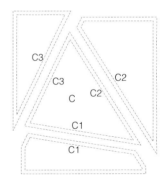

If you plan to use batiks, open up the bolt of fabric and look at a full yard of it before you buy it. Some batiks have large "muddy" spots where complementary colors have run into each other, leaving an unattractive grayish spot that is unusable in many quilts. If you love the fabric, buy a little extra and cut around it.

Love Beads

Skill level: simple ├──┼──③──┼──┤ advanced
Technical skills developed: precision cutting, using templates, piecing curves
Design skills developed: color selection, choosing quilting patterns
Size shown in photo: twin bed quilt

The name Love Beads conjures up vivid memories for those of us who grew up in the '60s. Some quilters might find the inset half circles of this quilt intimidating. If you take your time and follow our technique for piecing curves, you'll be amazed at how quickly you will master them. When looking for fabrics, be sure to choose a background fabric that doesn't show seams. Monochromatic, small-scale prints work well. Make sure that the fabrics used for the beads are not too similar in value to the background fabric, because you'll want the circles to read clearly. Because the circles are so strong and graphic, this is a quilt that can handle a playful approach to the quilting. You could use a contrasting thread or a playful stitch in the background, but quilt the beads tightly to give them texture.

finished size		wall	napping	twin	full/queen
size	*in (w x h)*	38 x 38	50 x 75	68 x 95	88 x 95
	cm	96 x 96	127 x 190	174 x 242	224 x 242
# of beads		13	14	18	22
FABRIC					
beads	assorted fabrics total				
	yards	1	1 ¼	1 ½	1 ½
	meters	1	1 ¼	1 ½	1 ½
string	fabrics total				
	yards	¼	¼	¼	¼
	meters	¼	¼	¼	¼
backgrounds	total				
	yards	1 ½	3 ½	5 ½	7
	meters	1 ½	3 ½	5	6 ½
backing	*yards*	1 ¼	3 ½	5 ½	8
	meters	1 ¼	3 ½	5	7 ½
binding	*yards*	½	¾	1	1
	meters	½	¾	1	1

In the sample, we chose to have multicolored beads, with each half a different color. Look how making each bead a single color changes the quilt. In the second variation, using an all-blue color palette with a white string draws attention to subtleties of color.

Further simplifying the color palette, the final two variations show how elegant the quilt becomes when you reduce the palette to three fabrics. The quilt also changes by making the beads lighter or darker than the background.

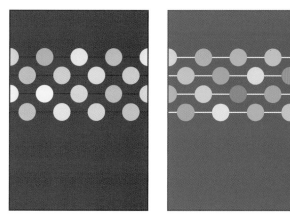
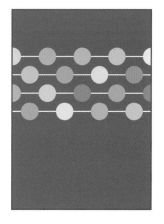
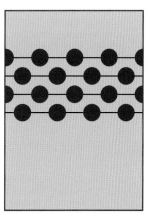
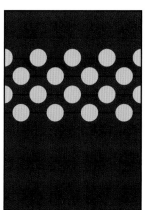

PIECES	wall	napping	twin	full/queen
semicircle **A**	26	28	36	44
9" x 9" **B** squares (23 x 23 cm)	26	28	36	44
9" x 8¾" **A** squares (23 x 22 cm)	4	7	9	11
1" x 9" string strips (2.5 x 23 cm)	12	14	18	22
background section 1	none	10" x 60" (25 x 152 cm)	14" x 77" (36 x 195 cm)	14" x 95" (36 x 241 cm)
background section 2	none	25" x 60" (64 x 152 cm)	40" x 77" (100 x 195 cm)	40" x 95" (100 x 241 cm)

Directions

1. Transfer the templates found in the appendix onto template plastic. (*Figure 1*)

2. Cut the specified number of semicircles from the various bead fabrics using template **A**.

3. Cut the specified number of squares from the background fabric.

4. Lay template **B** flush with one edge of a square, then cut out and discard the semicircle. Note that template **B** is smaller than the finished square—you're just using it to remove the semicircle. (*Figure 2*)

5. Repeat step 4 to make the specified number of **B** pieces.

6. Inset semicircles **A** into **B** pieces following the instructions for piecing curves detailed on page 93. (*Figure 3*)

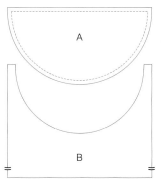

figure 1

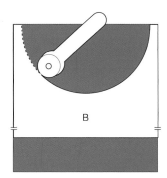

figure 2

48

We have ongoing debates in our classes about the role of quilting in a quilt. We strongly encourage all of our students to quilt their own quilts because we think that the quilting is such an important part of the quilt. Others say that it isn't fun for them or that they are intimidated at the thought of renting a long-arm quilting machine or attempting it on their home machine. Regardless of whether you do the quilting yourself or hire someone to do it, take the time to think about the role of the quilting in the quilt. Consider leaving the "string" unquilted to give it a different texture and more prominence. Sketch out some stitching patterns as we've done in these examples, and try to imagine the effect that different threads might have on the final piece. Attempt a sample of the quilting pattern you are considering on a scrap of the fabric with some batting. An 8" (20 cm) square of quilting will show you a lot. Wash it, dry it, and see if you like it. The quilting is really going to stand out in this quilt, so even if you don't do the quilting yourself, you'll be able to determine what it should look like.

7. Create a whole bead by pairing halves together, pinning through the edges of the circles to ensure proper alignment, then piecing. Iron open the seams. (*Figure 4*)

8. Cut the specified number of **C** pieces from the background fabric.

9. Lay out the beaded section of your quilt, placing a 1" x 9" (2.5 x 23 cm) strip between bead blocks. Use **C** pieces to fill in the gaps along the edges. (*Figure 5*)

10. Number the rows and piece blocks and strings together row by row.

11. Piece rows together, centering the strings of one row on the center of the beads of the row above or below. Iron open the seams.

12. Piece the remaining background sections and attach them to the beaded portion.

13. Layer the top, batting, and backing, then quilt. For more information on quilting, see "Making the Quilt," beginning on page 84.

14. Cut off the top and bottom halves of the beads to give the illusion that they continue off the quilt. This design technique, called engaging the edge, adds visual interest. (*Figure 6*)

15. Bind. For more information on binding, see page 103.

figure 3

figure 4

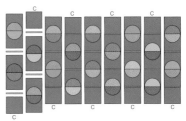

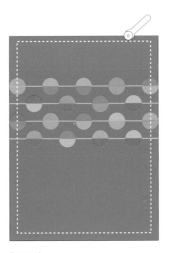

figure 6

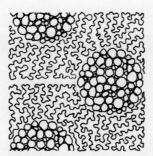

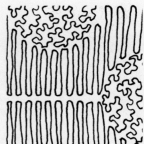

figure 5

Treehouse

Technical skills developed: piecing irregular forms, piecing in sequence, improvisational cutting
Design skills developed: color selection, composition
Size shown in photo: full/queen

When we first climbed the stairs to the master bedroom in our home, we were delighted to find that the large windows are at the same height as the canopy of the majestic maple tree that stands next to the house, making it feel as if we are sleeping in a treehouse. The morning light filtered through the leaves delights us daily and inspired us to make this quilt. This is a really fun and unusual quilt to make because you will be cutting and sewing four blocks at a time. You will need to follow the instructions carefully for the first few blocks, but once you get the idea, you will fly through the rest. For the "leaves," look for fabrics that are different values of one hue if you want a sparkly, luminous effect. Choose browns that are similar in hue and value for the "branches."

finished size		wall	napping	twin	full/queen
size	in (w x h)	35 x 49	49 x 73	63 x 98	84 x 98
	cm	90 x 126	126 x 189	162 x 252	216 x 252
blocks	w x h	5 x 4	7 x 6	9 x 8	12 x 8
FABRIC					
front	assorted greens				
	yards	1 ¾	3 ½	6	8
	meters	1 ¾	3 ½	5 ½	7 ½
front	assorted browns				
	yards	½	1	1 ½	2
	meters	½	1	1 ½	2
backing	yards	1 ½	3 ½	5 ½	8
	meters	1 ½	3 ½	5	7 ½
binding	yards	½	¾	1	1
	meters	½	¾	1	1

Variations

With so many random angles and piece sizes in this quilt, we suggest having a strong design intention when selecting the colors. We used just two hues—greens for the "leaves" and browns for the "branches." Imagine the view from this treehouse under a full moon in winter. The branches would be silhouetted in the bright moonlight. Or, what if you were looking out at sunset? Imagine the tree ablaze with color at the peak of autumn. Finally, put yourself in the treetops with colorful songbirds perched around you among the pale green leaves of spring.

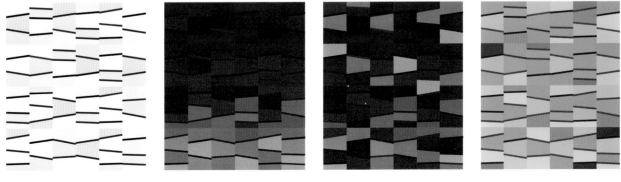

PIECES	wall	napping	twin	full/queen
7 ½" x 12 ¾" rectangles (19 x 32.5 cm)	20	60	96	132
1" x 40" strips (2.5 x 102 cm)	11	35	50	70

Directions

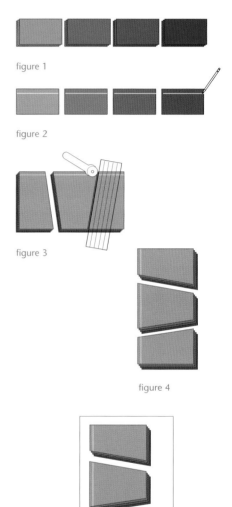

figure 1

figure 2

figure 3

figure 4

figure 5

1. Cut the green rectangles.

2. Sort the rectangles into four piles by value: light, medium, medium-dark, and dark. (*Figure 1*)

3. Cut the brown fabrics into 1" (2.5 cm) strips from selvage to selvage.

4. Select four rectangles, choosing from at least three different piles for a variety of values.

5. Chalk a line across the top of the four rectangles as shown in the illustration. These lines will help you remember which way is up. (*Figure 2*)

6. Stack the four rectangles precisely on top of each other, making sure they are perfectly aligned. Place a ruler on top of the stack according to the diagram and make angled cuts in two or three places from the top to the bottom edges. In our sample, we made two cuts in half of the blocks and three in the other half. Avoid cuts that create 90° angles. (*Figure 3*)

7. Taking care to keep all of the pieces together on the cutting mat, turn the blocks counterclockwise 90°. (*Figure 4*)

8. If you made two cuts, you will have three stacks of pieces. If you made three cuts, you will have four stacks. Take all but the stack closest to you (which will be the bottom piece of each block) to the sewing machine, along with various different brown strips. (*Figure 5*)

Design Tips

Composition is important in this quilt, so take your time thinking about how the blocks are going to look when they are pieced together. When possible, alternate darks and lights within a block, so no dark or light "holes" show up when you look at the quilt from across the room. Vary the angles and placement of the branches. Some should point up, and others down. Some cuts should be in the middle of the block, whereas others should be closer to the ends of the block. When you lay them out, check both the patterns created by the greens as well as those created by the browns to make sure you haven't unintentionally created any awkward spots. The bright greens lined up in the first example and the imbalance of lights and darks in the second should be avoided.

9. Using the chain-piecing method, place the green pieces face down along the brown strips with the chalk line away from you. Chain-piece, leaving a gap of 1" (2.5 cm) between each piece. (*Figure 6*) Use a variety of brown strips to give richness to the finished blocks.

10. Iron open the seams and trim the brown strips so they align with the edges of the green pieces. (*Figure 7*)

11. Lay out all of the pieces to form four blocks, making sure each block includes one of each of the different green fabrics. Pin together the individual blocks and chain-piece them until all four blocks are completed. (*Figure 8*)

12. Repeat steps 4 through 11 until all of the blocks are completed.

13. Lay out the blocks, chalking them in order, and piece them in rows. (*Figure 9*)

14. Piece together the rows.

15. Layer the top, batting, and backing, then quilt and bind. For more information on quilting and binding, see "Making the Quilt," beginning on page 84.

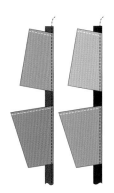

figure 6

figure 7

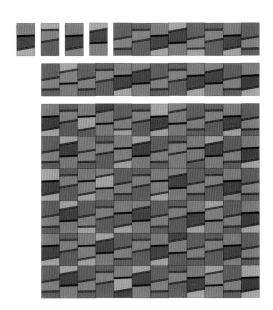

figure 9

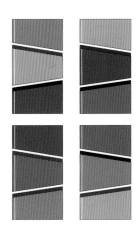

figure 8

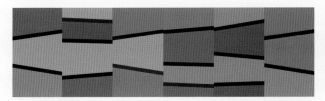

The light greens line up on the left creating a visual "hole"

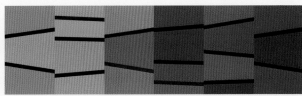

This row appears lopsided

Eclipse

Skill level: simple ⊢—┼—③—┼—⊣ advanced
Technical skills developed: piecing curves, working with templates
Design skills developed: understanding color, value, and composition
Size shown in photo: wall hanging

Eclipse, like our Prism fabrics designed for FreeSpirit, is an exploration of value, hue, and luminosity. It is shown here using most of the Prism fabrics.

Don't be intimidated by the circles. The large scale of the blocks makes piecing the curves simple. Even an adventurous beginner can make this quilt.

The elegant simplicity of Eclipse beckons you to experiment with color and fabric. This design lends itself equally well to prints, solids, and batiks. The variations shown on the following pages demonstrate the effects of changing the color palette.

finished size		wall	napping	twin	full/queen
size	in (w x h)	53 x 53	53 x 72	64 x 96	86 x 96
	cm	137 x 137	137 x 192	165 x 247	220 x 247
blocks	w x h	5 x 5	5 x 7	6 x 9	8 x 9
FABRIC					
squares	10 different fabrics				
	yards of each	½	¾	¾	1
	meters of each	½	¾	¾	1
arcs	10 different fabrics				
	yards of each	¼	¼	¼	½
	meters of each	¼	¼	¼	½
backing	yards	3	3 ½	5 ½	8
	meters	3	3 ½	5	7 ½
binding	yards	½	¾	1	1
	meters	½	¾	1	1

The Modern Quilt Workshop

Variations

You can make your quilt luminous by controlling the proportion of lights to mediums and darks. When choosing fabrics, select slightly different, but not overly contrasting, values for the circles and the squares. If you want to capture the luminous quality of the one shown, use two values of the same hue for each block, keeping the circles lighter and the fields slightly darker.

Another approach is to mix and match both hues and values. This arrangement will result in a playful quilt, but it won't have as much luminosity. Likewise, using dark circles on a light background will be striking but will have a very different feel. Note how calm this quilt becomes when made with analogous colors in the red and brown variations.

Remember, there is no right or wrong way to put this together, so experiment until you are happy with the colors. If you make a block that doesn't seem to fit, set it aside and try a new one.

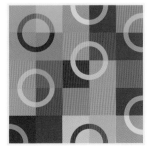   

PIECES	wall	napping	twin	full/queen
B arcs	21	28	41	54
11¼" x 11¼" **D** squares	25	35	54	72
(28.5 x 28.5 cm)				

Directions

This quilt comprises two types of blocks: whole squares and arc blocks (squares with inset quarter-circle bands). Precise cutting is essential to piecing curves successfully. Take your time and use a rotary cutter with a sharp blade. If any of your piecing is off, remember that the seam ripper is your friend—just take out the seam and try again. It will make the quilt go together more smoothly.

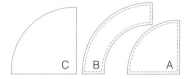

1. Transfer the templates found in the appendix onto template plastic.

2. Cut the **D** squares. You do not have to cut an equal number of each color. Variety will add visual interest.

3. To make the arc blocks, place template **C** in the corner of one of the squares and cut carefully along the curve. (*Figure 1*)

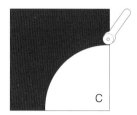

figure 1

4. Place template **A** in the corner of the quarter circle you just removed from the square. (*Figure 2*)

5. Cut along the template and discard the thin arc. Pin the two remaining pieces together. (*Figure 3*)

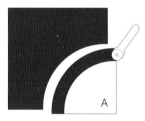

figure 2

6. Repeat steps 3 and 4 for as many squares as there are arcs. (Some squares will remain uncut.)

figure 3

Design Tips

Although this quilt may appear minimal, the subtle shifts in value make it dynamic. What makes it even more interesting is that the circles appear only at some of the intersections of the squares. Your eye does not get stuck on one area of the quilt but rather keeps moving. In addition, certain circles get cut off at the edge—known as "engaging the edge"—which frees your mind to imagine the quilt continuing into space. For more on engaging the edge, see "Where have all the borders gone?" on page 14.

Whether you are making a wall hanging or a bed quilt from this pattern, use the opportunity to explore composition. The blocks can be arranged in many ways. Take your time laying it out to develop a composition that is both pleasing and dynamic.

Notice that differences in the composition change the feel of the quilt. Pay close attention to the difference between the variations that are "randomly" composed and those that are carefully ordered.

7. Cut the arcs using template **B**.

8. Match the arcs with the paired sets. (*Figure 4*)

9. Piece the arcs to the quarter circles, following the instructions for piecing curves found on page 93. (*Figure 5*)

10. Match the pieced quarter circle and arc combination to the main block. (*Figure 6*)

11. Piece the quarter-circle and arc combination to the main block (*Figure 7*)

12. Lay out your blocks. Shift the blocks around until you like the composition.

13. Sew together: first sew the individual rows using the leapfrogging technique described on pages 91–92, then sew all the rows together. To ensure accurate piecing, align your seams with pins. (*Figure 8*)

14. Layer the top, batting, and backing, then quilt and bind. For more information on quilting and binding, see "Making the Quilt," beginning on page 84.

figure 4

figure 5

figure 6

figure 7

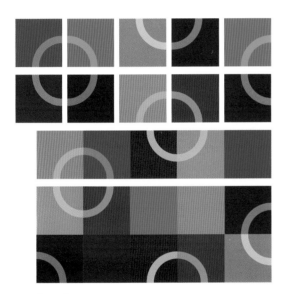

figure 8

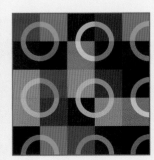

Book Club

Skill level: simple ├──┼──④──┼──┤ advanced
Technical skills developed: piecing strips
Design skills developed: composition, color selection
Size shown in photo: wall hanging

A world of inspiration can be found at your local library. We designed the Book Club quilt to honor the books that have inspired us throughout the years. This quilt is a fun project for quilters who hate to match points but who like clean lines. It is also an appropriate segue for people who have never done anything improvisational but are yearning to try something new. When choosing fabrics for this design, avoid high-contrast patterns or large-scale prints. Choose fabrics of a similar saturation so none seem more dominant than the others. Select fabrics for the books that are different in value from the background color, so the forms of the books will read clearly. If you have a directional fabric such as a stripe, cut it so the pattern is perpendicular to the long edge of the books and use it on a thinner book.

finished size		wall	napping	twin	full/queen
size	*in (w x h)*	38 x 48	48 x 80	66 x 96	86 x 96
	cm	96 x 122	122 x 203	167 x 243	218 x 243
# of shelves		3	5	6	6
FABRIC					
bookshelf	assorted fabrics total				
	yards	1 ¾	3 ¼	5	7
	meters	1 ¾	3	4 ½	6 ½
backgrounds	total				
	yards	1 ½	3 ¼	5	6 ½
	meters	1 ½	3	4 ½	6
backing	*yards*	1 ¼	3 ½	5 ½	8
	meters	1 ¼	3 ½	5	7 ½
shelves &	*yards*	½	¾	1	1 ½
binding	*meters*	½	¾	1	1 ¼

Variations

Here are three shelves of books. Simply by changing the color palette, you can imagine that the first shelf sits in a wood-paneled law firm library. The second shelf of books could be in any child's bedroom, full of slim yet colorful storybooks. The final shelf has the variety you might expect in a public library.

PIECES	wall	napping	twin	full/queen
book strips should be between 1" (2.5 cm) and 3¼" (8.5 cm) wide and between 8½" (21 cm) and 13" (33 cm) high				
book strips (approx.)	70	160	250	320
9" x 40" background **A** (23 x 102 cm)	5	10	17	24

Directions

1. Begin by making the leaning books. For each book, sew 3" (7.5 cm) -wide strips to the sides, then to the top of a book strip. (*Figure 1*)

2. Tilt the block slightly to one side. Trim the bottom ¼" (0.5 cm) from the bottom corner of the book. (*Figure 2*)

3. Trim left side ¼" (0.5 cm) from the top corner of the book and perpendicular to the bottom cut. (*Figure 3*)

4. Trim the right side ¼" (0.5 cm) from the other bottom corner of the book and perpendicular to the bottom cut. (*Figure 4*)

5. Trim the top edge ¼" (0.5 cm) from the other top corner of the book and parallel to the bottom cut. (*Figure 5*)

6. Cut fabric strips for books. Make one or two of the book strips the same color as the background—this will let you create gaps between the books or at the end of the shelves. The strips should vary in size from a minimum width of 1" (2.5 cm) to a maximum width of 3 ¼" (8 cm), and from a minimum height of 8 ½" (21 cm) to a maximum height of 13" (33 cm).

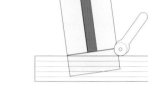

figure 1

figure 2

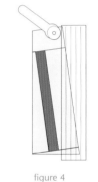

figure 3

figure 4

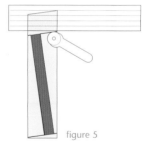

figure 5

Design Tips

When composing the shelves of books, think about the impact of the colors you have selected. The lightest, darkest, and most saturated colors in your palette are going to stand out more than the more muted, medium-value fabrics. To balance the impact of the various colors, use the strongest fabrics for the thinnest, smallest books in your quilt. Conversely, using the more subtle colors in larger amounts will balance the impact of the stronger colors. Try to alternate the books so the smaller ones are interspersed nicely with the larger ones on the shelf. Once you have completed each shelf, determine which has the most number of big books and use it on the bottom of the quilt. The shelf that has the lightest feel to it visually should go on top. This will prevent the quilt from looking top-heavy.

7. Sew the book strips and the tilting book strips to background fabric **A**, as shown. (*Figure 6*)

8. Iron open the seams and trim flush into individual pieces. (*Figure 7*)

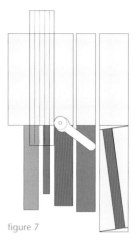

figure 6

9. Lay out the books one shelf at a time. Because you will lose a lot of width to the seam allowance, your shelf will be nearly twice as wide when you lay it out as after you piece it together. Move the individual books up or down to get a variety of heights. Make sure the leaning books lean against taller books.

10. Chalk a line that will become the bookshelf ¼" (0.5 cm) below the bottom corner of the leaning books. Chalk another line 16½" (42 cm) from the bottom. Trim on the lines, then piece together the books. (*Figure 8*)

11. Piece together the shelves, sewing a 1" (2.5 cm) strip between each row of books to form the bookshelf. Use the same fabric for the binding as for the shelves to form the outer edges of the bookshelf. (*Figure 9*)

12. Layer the top, batting, and backing, then quilt and bind. For more information on quilting and binding, see "Making the Quilt," beginning on page 84.

figure 7

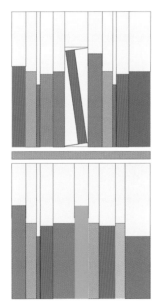

figure 9

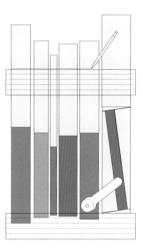

figure 8

Patterns

61

The thin books are bright, giving a balanced feel

The thick books are too bright, drawing too much attention

Gamelan

Technical skills developed: precision cutting and piecing, piecing curves
Design skills developed: working with bilaterally symmetrical fabrics, understanding repeats
Size shown in photo: napping

When our dear friend moved to Indonesia, we sent her $50 and asked her to buy us some local textiles. She sent us a bundle of beautiful fabrics, all of which had large, bilaterally symmetrical repeats. We loved them but weren't immediately sure how best to use them. Finally, we designed this quilt, which uses the large repeats to their best advantage, creating breathtaking kaleidoscopic patterns. We named it Gamelan, after the traditional Indonesian orchestra composed of drums, gongs, and xylophones.

After working with the large-scale, bilaterally symmetrical fabrics used in this quilt, we decided to add some to our Prism fabric line, and thus the Prism Imagine series was born. The Prism Imagine series works beautifully with this pattern, as do many traditional border prints. Just check to make sure that they are perfectly symmetrical.

finished size		wall	napping	twin	full/queen
size	in (w x h)	34 x 34	50 x 80	65 x 93	86 x 94
	cm	86 x 86	127 x 203	165 x 237	219 x 239
# of circles		3	7	8	8
FABRIC					
circle	You will need enough bilaterally symmetrical fabric to cut out 8 indentical wedges per circle.				
backgrounds	total				
	yards	1 ½	3 ½	5 ½	7
	meters	1 ½	3 ½	5	6 ½
backing	yards	1 ½	3 ½	5 ½	8
	meters	1 ½	3 ½	5	7 ½
binding	yards	½	¾	1	1
	meters	½	¾	1	1

Variations

This is a fabric-dependent design, so rather than show color variations with fabrics you probably can't find, we've chosen to show compositional variations using the basic block of a pieced circle. Whether laid out in a grid or aligned horizontally like a plate rail, this technique will produce a stunning quilt.

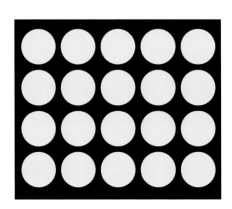

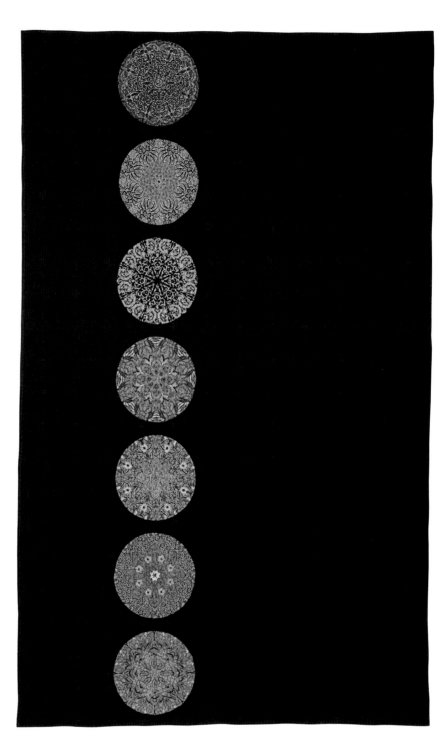

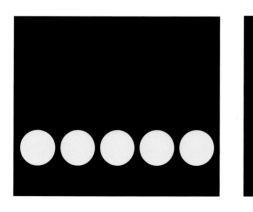

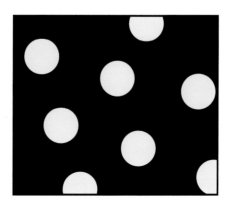

PIECES	wall	napping	twin	full/queen
wedges	24	56	64	64
6 ¼" x 6 ¼" squares (16 x 16 cm)	12	28	32	32
side strip 1	9" x 35" (20 x 89 cm)	11" x 81" (28 x 206 cm)	19" x 92" (48 x 234 cm)	27" x 92" (69 x 234 cm)
side strip 2	14" x 35" (36 x 89 cm)	28" x 81" (71 x 206 cm)	65" x 92" (165 x 234 cm)	122" x 92" (69 x 234 cm)

Directions

1. Transfer the templates found in the appendix onto template plastic, marking the seam allowances and centerline of the wedge-shaped template. (*Figure 1*)

2. Place a loop of tape on the underside of the templates to prevent them from shifting when you cut your fabric.

3. Using the corner template, cut the specified number of corner pieces from your background squares.

4. Lay out your ironed, bilaterally symmetrical fabric, and find the axis of symmetry in the repeat (see Design Tips below for more on locating the axis). Select the portion of the repeat that you want to use, making sure that you have enough of the fabric to cut the repeat eight times. As you make your selection, remember that the outside ¼" (0.5 cm) will be hidden in the seam allowance.

5. Place the wedge template on the fabric, precisely aligning the centerline of the template with the axis of the repeat. Using a permanent marker, trace part of the fabric pattern onto the template so you'll be able to align the template with the repeat when cutting the other pieces. (*Figure 2*)

6. Cut the first piece. (*Figure 3*)

7. Find the exact same part of the repeat on other sections of the fabric and cut the remaining pieces. Although you might be tempted to try to cut several pieces at one time by stacking the repeats, beware of doing so, because even the smallest slip in the layers will make it difficult, if not impossible, to match the repeats when it's time to piece.

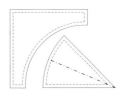

figure 1

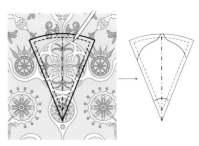

figure 2

figure 3

Design Tips

Bilaterally symmetrical fabrics have an axis that runs down the center of the repeat, with the design on the left side of the axis an exact mirror image of the design on the right side of the image. Bilaterally symmetrical fabrics can be hard to find because they must be designed with great precision. If you want the pattern to work, however, you must use fabrics that are designed this way. These first two examples are from our Prism Imagine fabric line.

Bilaterally symmetrical

Bilaterally symmetrical

8. Pin pairs of the pieces together, making sure that the fabric patterns align ¼" (0.5 cm) from the raw edge, where the seam will be. Piece them together. (*Figure 4*)

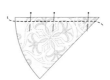

figure 4

9. Iron open the seams. The pairs you've just sewn should now be quarter circles. (*Figure 5*)

figure 5

10. Inset the quarter circles into the block corners following the instructions for piecing curves found on page 93. (*Figure 6*). Repeat to make four sets.

11. Pinning carefully to align the patterns at the seam, piece together two sets to make half circles. Iron open the seams. (*Figure 7*)

figure 6

12. Piece together the halves to make a full circle. Iron open the seams. (*Figure 8*)

13. Repeat for the remaining circles.

14. Piece all of the circles together into a column and iron open the seams. (*Figure 9*)

15. Piece together the remaining background and attach to the circles.

16. Layer the top, batting, and backing, then quilt and bind. For more information on quilting and binding, see "Making the Quilt," beginning on page 84.

figure 7

figure 9

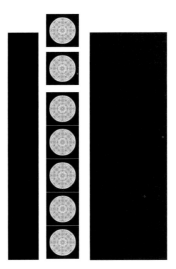

figure 8

Patterns

65

Some fabrics appear bilaterally symmetrical, but if they are off even slightly, they won't work. Once you find them, buy a lot of yardage because you will need to cut identical parts of the same repeat. Some fabrics have multiple axes, giving you greater selection. You can often make different kaleidoscopes from the same fabric just by selecting a different part of the repeat.

Not quite bilaterally symmetrical

Not quite bilaterally symmetrical

Boomerang

Skill level: simple ├──┼──┼──┤⑤ advanced
Technical skills developed: precision cutting, working with templates, precision piecing
Design skills developed: color selection, discerning values
Size shown in photo: wall hanging

This quilt is all about transparency. The colors are chosen to make the boomerangs appear transparent when they overlap. Although this is a technically challenging quilt because it requires precision in cutting, piecing, and ironing, it is a wonderful project for the quilter who wants to learn a new way of seeing and thinking about color. Boomerang is an excellent reminder that the workhorse fabrics in a complex quilt often are not the ones that scream at you from across the room but rather the quiet fabrics that are easy to overlook. Take your time looking for fabrics—you may find the perfect ones already in your stash. When looking for fabric, choose low-contrast, tone-on-tone prints in distinctly different value ranges to achieve the effect of transparency. See Design Tips (pages 68–69) for more on fabric selection.

finished size		wall	napping	twin	full/queen
size	*in (w x h)*	40 x 40	48 x 80	64 x 96	88 x 96
	cm	102 x 102	122 x 204	163 x 244	224 x 244
blocks	*w x h*	5 x 5	6 x 10	8 x 12	11 x 12
FABRIC					
boomerang	fabrics total				
	yards	1¾	4	6¾	8½
	meters	1¾	3¾	6	7
overlap	fabrics total				
	yards	½	¾	1	1½
	meters	½	¾	1	1½
backgrounds	total				
	yards	2	5	7¼	10
	meters	2	4½	7	9¼
backing	*yards*	1½	3½	5½	8
	meters	1½	3½	5	7½
binding	*yards*	½	¾	1	1
	meters	½	¾	1	1

Variations

The goal in choosing colors is to achieve a sense of transparency. Keep the background fairly calm. Stick to a narrow range of hues and values, as shown in the purple, blue, and orange examples. You can also use a single fabric, as shown in the black and the white examples. For the boomerangs themselves you can use analogous colors or you can experiment with variety, as shown in the white quilt with pastel boomerangs.

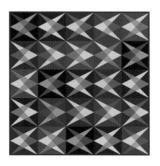

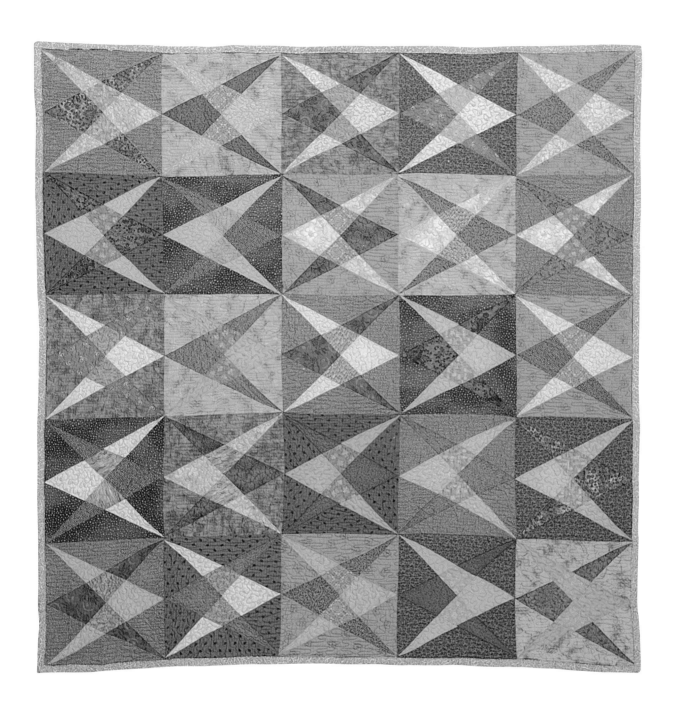

PIECES	wall	napping	twin	full/queen
boomerang **A**	50	120	192	264
boomerang **B + C**	100	240	384	528
overlap **E**	50	120	192	264
background **F**	50	120	192	264
background **G**	50	120	192	264
background **H**	50	120	192	264

Directions

To achieve a rich look, we suggest using at least seven fabrics for each of the background, the boomerang, and the overlap colors. Boomerang is a quilt that requires careful cutting and piecing to maintain the points of the boomerang forms. If you haven't pieced triangles before, read the section on how to pin and piece accurately, in "Creating the Quilt," beginning on page 78. We recommend making a block at a time until you are comfortable with the process. With experience, you might choose to cut and piece several blocks at a time.

1. Transfer the templates found in the appendix onto template plastic. *Figure 1* shows the structure of the block.

2. For each block, begin by choosing four fabrics: a background, two different boomerang fabrics, and one overlap fabric (see Design Tips).

3. For each block, cut two pieces each of the background fabric with templates **F**, **G**, and **H**. Pieces can be easily confused, so label them with chalk.

4. From the first boomerang fabric, cut one piece with template **A**, one with template **B**, and one with template **C**.

5. From the second boomerang fabric, cut one piece with template **A**, one with template **B**, and one with template **C**.

6. Cut two pieces from the overlap fabric with template **E**.

7. Piece together pairs in the sequence shown. (*Figure 2*)

8. If you've never pieced thin triangles, this may take patience. Look at *figure 3* to better understand alignment. When piecing

figure 1

figure 2

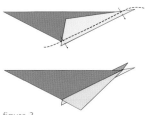

figure 3

Design Tips

Choose two colors for the points of the boomerangs. Look closely at the colors you have chosen. Imagine the color that would fall in between the two colors you have chosen and find it in your stash. If you have difficulty finding the exact colors you need, ask friends to swap some scraps. Because the blocks are small and can all be different, even a small amount of the perfect fabric can make a difference. In the sample quilt, we chose various golden yellows and muted oranges. The in-between color is an orangey yellow of similar value. For the field color, we chose different shades of olive green. Olive green is a complementary color to any orange tone, so we knew that the boomerang form would read clearly. Note also that we changed thread colors when quilting so the boomerang form would be further differentiated from the background.

together the triangles, imagine where the finished ¼" (0.5 cm) seams end and pin. Iron all the seams open. The seams will become too bulky if they aren't ironed open.

9. Finish piecing the quarter squares. (*Figure 4*). Lay the pieced triangles down to make sure they lie flat and fit together. If any of the triangles are badly distorted or don't lie flat, you may have accidentally mixed up templates **F** and **G** or templates **B** and **C**.

10. To make halves, align the quarters by pinning through the seams. Piece, then iron the seams open. (*Figure 5*)

11. To complete the squares, align the halves by pinning through the seams. Piece, then iron the seams open. (*Figure 6*)

12. Repeat steps 2 through 11 to make the desired number of blocks.

13. Lay out your blocks, paying attention to adjacencies. Try to avoid having the same background colors edge to edge. Note that in the example pictured, we have the orange boomerangs alternating direction in each row. We did this to emphasize the nature of a boomerang—you throw it one way, then it comes back to you.

14. Piece together the blocks to form rows and iron the seams open. (*Figure 7*). Piece the rows together, then iron the seams open.

15. Layer the top, batting, and backing, then quilt and bind. For more information on quilting and binding, see "Making the Quilt," beginning on page 84.

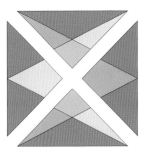
figure 4

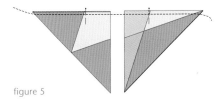
figure 5

figure 6

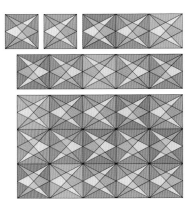
figure 7

Pink and blue boomerangs would overlap with lavender

Pink and violet boomerangs would overlap with red-violet

Yellow and blue boomerangs would overlap with green

Green and yellow boomerangs would overlap with yellow-green

XOXO

Skill level: simple ⊢——⊢——⊢——⊢——⊢(5)——⊢ advanced
Technical skills developed: precision cutting, using templates, piecing curves
Design skills developed: color selection, differentiating values
Size shown in photo: wall hanging

We first developed this block as part of our daughter's baby quilt. We loved the abstraction of the XOXO used in the closing of correspondence to represent hugs and kisses and thought it would be a playful yet meaningful block for a loved one. Although the design of the XOXO quilt requires precision in cutting, pinning, piecing, and ironing, it is a welcome challenge for quilters who are tired of the same old squares, triangles and stars. If you have never pieced curves before, be sure to make a sample block before you start. When you are ready to quilt, choose a quilting thread color that is similar in value or halfway between the value of the Xs and the Os. A contrasting thread color would be distracting for such a complex block.

finished size		wall	napping	twin	full/queen
size	*in (w x h)*	42 x 42	51 x 76	68 x 93	85 x 93
	cm	106 x 106	130 x 193	173 x 237	216 x 237
blocks	*w x h*	5 x 5	6 x 9	8 x 11	10 x 11
FABRIC					
x	fabrics total				
	yards	¾	1 ¼	1 ¾	2 ¼
	meters	¾	1 ¼	1 ¾	2 ¼
o	fabrics total				
	yards	1 ¾	3	5	6
	meters	1 ¾	3	5	5 ½
backgrounds	total				
	yards	1 ½	2 ½	3 ¾	4 ¾
	meters	1 ½	2 ¼	3 ½	4 ½
backing	*yards*	1 ½	3 ½	5 ½	8
	meters	1 ½	3 ½	5	7 ½
binding	*yards*	½	¾	1	1
	meters	½	¾	1	1

Variations

When choosing your colors, consider the relationship among the three main elements: the background, the circles, and the diagonal lattice. Notice how the differences in value and hue among these elements change the feel of the quilt. The first two variations show analogous color palettes of yellows, oranges, and reds. The first example is gentle, with its autumnal feel and wide variation of colors used for the circles. The second example is more graphic, using just three different fabrics. The third example also uses just three fabrics, but because they are of similar hues and values, the design is much calmer. The final example shows multicolored circles, which infuse the quilt with a dynamic feel.

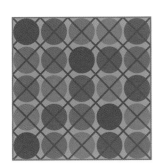
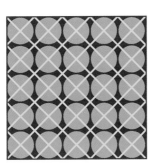
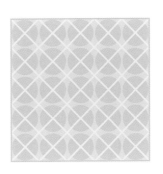
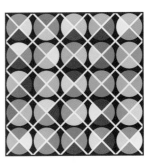

PIECES	wall	napping	twin	full/queen
quarter circle **A**	100	216	352	440
piece **B**	100	216	352	440
1" x 40" strips (2.5 x 102 cm)	18	38	60	74

Directions

1. Transfer the templates found in the appendix onto template plastic. Cut out the specified number of pieces of **A** and **B**. (*Figure 1*)

2. Cut the 1" x 40" (2.5 x 102 cm) strips that will form the Xs.

3. Lay out the **A** and **B** pieces into blocks. (*Figure 2*)

4. Piece **A** to **B**, following the instructions for piecing curves found on page 93, and iron open the seams. (*Figure 3*)

5. Strip-piece the strips to two of the quarter circles in each block. (*Figure 4*)

6. Iron the seams open and trim the pieces. (*Figure 5*)

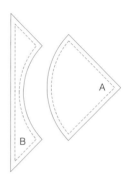

figure 1

figure 2

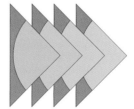

figure 3

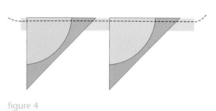

figure 4

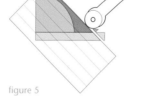

figure 5

Design Tips

When selecting fabrics for this design, look carefully for fabrics of similar value for the Xs and the Os. If you are buying new fabric or combining new fabric with some from your stash, place them all in a pile in the quilt shop and walk across the room to look at them from a distance. If you wear glasses, take them off and see whether the fabrics blend together nicely.

A subtle tone-on-tone print would work well with this pattern

This high-contrast print would not work well

7. Piece the other quarter circle to the strip to form a half circle. Iron the seams open. (*Figure 6*)

8. Strip-piece one of the half circles from each block to the remaining strips.

9. Mark perpendicular lines across the strip from the center strip and the endpoints. These help you line up the other half. (*Figure 7*). Iron open the seams.

10. Pin the remaining half circles to the strips, taking care to align them with the chalk marks. (*Figure 8*)

11. Sew the seams, then iron them open.

12. Trim the squares. (*Figure 9*)

13. Lay out and piece together all of the blocks. (*Figure 10*)

14. Layer the top, batting, and backing, then quilt and bind. For more information on quilting and binding, see "Making the Quilt," beginning on page 84.

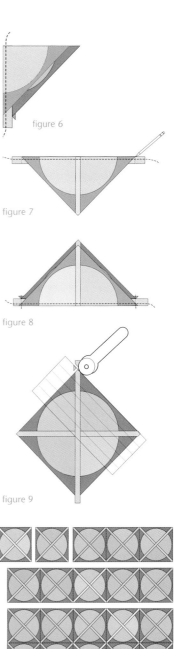

figure 6

figure 7

figure 8

figure 9

figure 10

If they do, then they are of similar value and hue. If any of them "pop," remove them and look for something else. You will also want to look for tone-on-tone fabrics or other low-contrast prints. They will not compete with the design of the block and will help the edges of the circles read crisply.

This high-contrast print would not work well either

Unfinished Business

Skill level: simple ├──┼──┼──┼──⑤──┤ advanced
Technical skills developed: improvisational cutting and piecing
Design skills developed: understanding value, color selection, composition
Size shown in photo: wall hanging

We designed Unfinished Business as a contemporary interpretation of a crazy quilt, but with luminous color work that gives the quilt added sophistication. We love the contrast between the chaos of the piecing and the clean lines of the colored bands. This quilt is pieced using improvisational cutting and piecing, which is described in detail below. The "improvisational" part of it means that we can't tell you exactly how many strips of which color you will need and how wide your blocks need to be. This will depend on whether you are trying to incorporate scraps and how big you decide to cut your pieces. As long as you have a finished band that is your desired height and width for each color, it doesn't matter how you get there. If you hate to match points and prefer to make it up as you go, this quilt is a lot of fun. It is also, however, very time consuming because it requires lots of small pieces and plenty of cutting and ironing.

finished size		wall	napping	twin	full/queen
size	*in (w x h)*	40 x 40	48 x 75	63 x 95	88 x 95
	cm	100 x 100	122 x 190	160 x 245	224 x 245
FABRIC					
front	per colorband				
	yards	1 ¾	4	6 ½	9
	meters	1 ¾	3 ¾	6	8 ½
backing	*yards*	1 ½	3 ½	5 ½	8
	meters	1 ½	3 ½	5	7 ½
binding	*yards*	½	¾	1	1
	meters	½	¾	1	1

Variations

Although changing fabrics transforms some quilts, making this into a series of vertical, not horizontal, bands changes this as well. Turning it upside down also changes it dramatically. You can even transform the design by shifting value rather than hue. The original quilt shifts in hue from yellow to orange to burgundy. These examples of reds, blue-greens, and grays show value shifts from light to dark.

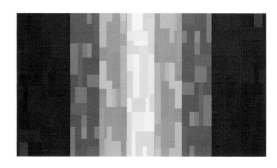

PIECES	wall	napping	twin	full/queen
building block height	8½" (21 cm)	15½" (39 cm)	19½" (50 cm)	19½" (50 cm)
finished bands	8½" x 40" (21 x 100 cm)	15½" x 48" (39 x 122 cm)	19½" x 63" (50 x 160 cm)	19½" x 88" (50 x 224 cm)

Directions

1. Divide your fabrics into piles by value.

2. Start with the lightest color. If you are working with scraps, trim the long, thin ones into strips the length of the scrap and between 1" and 3" (2.5–7.5 cm) wide. (*Figure 1*)

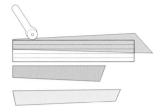

figure 1

3. Take the scraps that are squarish in shape and trim them into irregular four-sided shapes no longer than 4" (10 cm) on any side. (*Figure 2*)

figure 2

4. If you are using new fabric, first cut strips from selvage to selvage that are between 2" and 4" (5–10 cm) wide. Then, cutting at varied angles, cut irregular, four-sided shapes. (*Figure 3*). Also cut some long strips that are between 1" and 3" (2.5–7.5 cm) wide.

5. You will now be making blocks that are all the specified height (for instance, 8½" [21 cm] for the wall hanging) and of various widths. Some of your blocks may be 5" (12.5 cm) wide, and some could be 15" (38 cm) wide.

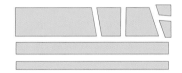

figure 3

6. Strip-piece five of your irregular four-sided shapes onto the thin strips. If you are using scraps, use the shortest strips first, because you'll need the longer ones later. (*Figure 4*). Iron open the seams.

7. Placing your ruler along the edge of the piece, trim the strips flush, as shown. We'll call these pieces the "centers." Set them aside. (*Figure 5*)

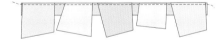

figure 4

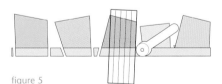

figure 5

Design Tips

This quilt is the perfect project for scrap-savers like us. Much of the work in this quilt is deciding on fabric choices, so the more you have to work with the better. Some batiks work well, but tone-on-tone, small-scale prints are easiest. Even tiny pieces work beautifully. Scour your quilting guilds and ask friends for scraps, if necessary. Before you make your final fabric choices, place them on a wall and look at them from the other side of the room, following what we refer to as the Ten-Foot Rule. From ten feet away you will be able to see whether the colors blend nicely and whether there is enough, or perhaps too much, contrast between the bands. If you need to look for some supplemental fabrics, be sure to take all of the scraps with you to the fabric store, because colors always look different at home than they do in the store. Consider switching thread colors when you quilt so each of the bands will maintain its vibrancy. If you know where you'll be using this quilt, take your fabric scraps to that room to look at them in place.

8. Piece together some of the long and/or short strips along the long edge. Iron the seams open. (*Figure 6*)

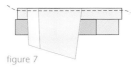
figure 6

9. Strip-piece some of the centers to the long strips you have just sewn. (*Figure 7*) Iron and trim. (*Figure 8*)

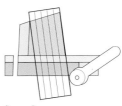
figure 7

10. Continue to build up the centers by adding strips to them or by sewing together two centers. Trim the larger pieces so they can be sewn to smaller pieces, or build up smaller pieces with strips until they can be sewn to larger pieces. Trim and iron after each seam. Try to work on several centers at a time so you can proceed efficiently. (*Figure 9*)

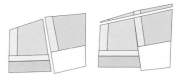
figure 8

11. When you have pieces that are at least the specified height on one side, trim the edges along the grid of your cutting mat so you have a perfect 90° rectangle that is the specified height (for instance 8 1/2" [21 cm] for the wall hanging) on two sides and any other dimension on the other two sides. Set the piece aside and repeat the same process on the other centers until you have enough rectangles to get the width of the finished quilt. (*Figure 10*)

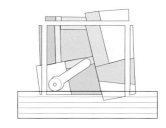
figure 9

12. Sew all of the rectangles together into a band and iron open the seams. (*Figure 11*)

13. Use these same techniques for the remaining bands. Be sure the seams are staggered when you assemble the bands.

14. Piece the bands together and iron the seams open.

15. Layer the top, batting, and backing, then quilt and bind. For more information on quilting and binding, see "Making the Quilt," beginning on page 84.

figure 10

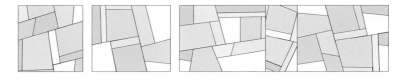
figure 11

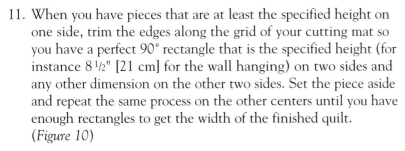

We keep all our small scraps sorted by color in transparent boxes

Creating the Quilt

Designing the Quilt

Designing the quilt is the most important step in the process of making a quilt. No matter how exquisite your craftsmanship may be, if your color and fabric choices don't work, you're stuck with a beautifully made yet unappealing quilt. On the other hand, there are many beautiful, frequently published, award-winning quilts whose beauty overcomes the poor craftsmanship evident upon closer inspection.

In our classes and in our first book, *Color Harmony for Quilts*, we encourage students to come up with a Big Idea before they set foot in the quilt shop, even if they plan to use a standard pattern. The Big Idea refers to a design intention or a design inspiration for the quilt. Sometimes the Big Idea is a wonderful memory from a special family trip, or a reminder of a mood that you'd like to set in your home. Having a Big Idea helps you make color decisions so you don't have that deer-in-headlights look once you are surrounded by 5,000 bolts of beautiful fabric. If you have a Big Idea before you walk in the shop, you will have already narrowed down your choices to less than 10 percent of the fabric in the shop. If you are trying to match a specific color already in your house, a large safety pin with the paint chips and upholstery swatches used in your home is a great thing to take to your quilt shop. If you're on the lookout for a specific fabric, keep a safety pin with a couple of compatible swatches in your purse or wallet.

Let's say you want to make the Zipper quilt on page 38. We've made the sample in soothing blues and greens, but your color selection could turn it into a bright, cheery quilt suitable for a child's bedroom or a rich, sophisticated palette appropriate for a family room. Here are some questions to ask yourself to help you develop a Big Idea. Where is the quilt going to be used? What adjective would you choose to describe the role of that quilt in the room? Is it cheery, peaceful, festive, sophisticated, homey? What memories do you associate with that adjective? Here are some examples of color palettes our students developed and the Big Ideas they express:

Kelly greens, grassy greens, and mossy gray selected from memories of the ubiquitous stone walls and rolling hills seen on a family trip to Ireland

Muted earth tones with golds, greens, and blues seen on a familiar drive through the Midwest prairie to visit an elderly mother

Vivid shades of pinks, reds, and oranges favored by a friend who loved wearing bright shades of lipstick

A chocolate brown, red, and hot pink combination capturing the spirit of a vivacious but out-of-control new puppy

An olive green and purple palette recalling a father who served in the military and the wines he loved from his Italian heritage

Sometimes students come in with a specific fabric they are dying to use, so we work backward to define what it is about that fabric that they find so compelling. Usually it reminds them of something or invokes some positive feeling in them. We talk it through until a Big Idea starts to develop. The Big Idea helps you decide what you want the tone of the quilt to be. Having the colors in your quilt tied to a Big Idea will help you make better design decisions and help you make quilts that are unique to you and your life experiences.

Inky blues and golds for one student who wanted to capture the moonlight when she worked the "graveyard shift" telecommuting from her home office

Fabric Selection— The Secret Life of Fabric

"Overwhelmed!" This is the response we most frequently hear when a first-time quilter makes a trip to a quilt shop. Many new quilters walk into a quilt shop expecting to have a half-dozen compatible fabrics jump out at them, making their fabric selections obvious and fail-proof. The reality is that most quilt shops have thousands of bolts in inventory, which can make fabric selection harder rather than easier.

Monochromatic print fabric

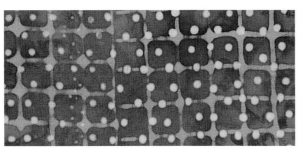

Batik fabric

Solid fabric

At most quilt shops you will find the following types of fabrics: multicolored prints, large-patterned prints, monochromatic prints, batiks, and solids. Although most quilt shops divide

their displays according to color or designer, you should train yourself to look at a bolt and anticipate how it would be used in a quilt. For example, if it is a large-patterned print, it probably would not be a good choice for a binding. Conversely, a small-scale print used as the backing for a king-size bed quilt might look dull and uninspired.

It is so easy to fall in love with a bolt of fabric. Its sophisticated colors beckon you from across the fabric shop, luring you into the belief that if you just had this fabric in your stash, all of your quilts would be unfailingly beautiful. Sometimes these fabrics really do transform your quilts as you knew they would, and sometimes they just sit folded up in the stash, unable or unwilling to play well with your other fabrics. As in love, it is sometimes the shy, overlooked fabrics in the corner that are the reliable participants in your quilts. When it comes to choosing fabrics, the first step is learning to discern the difference between love and infatuation. Fabrics can be beautiful in a display or on a bolt, but if they aren't flexible enough to work with other fabrics in your stash, you won't end up using them.

That is not to say that you shouldn't buy fabrics that you love. But first, try to imagine them with five or six other fabrics. How will they look cut up in small pieces? Sometimes large-patterned fabrics look great on the bolt but are harder to use in combination with other fabrics. Occasionally they appear to overwhelm smaller-scale prints. In other instances, large-patterned fabrics can prevent a simple quilt from becoming too plain.

A good rule of thumb is to think about the design of the quilt first. Is it a simple pattern with one basic form (squares, triangles, circles, and so on)? If so, it can support a variety of colors and patterns. If it is a more complex design with lots of different forms, or if you plan to use a broad variety of colors, you are better off sticking to low-contrast, monochromatic prints or solids.

Another often-overlooked aspect of fabric is contrast. Students frequently bring in a pile of fabrics that they think "match" one another. There might be one multicolored fabric with a high-contrast pattern (see right, top image). Then there might be a low-contrast, monochromatic print. If each of these fabrics is to be used in equal amounts, the high-contrast fabric will "pop," and the low-contrast fabric will recede to the background. White is often the culprit here. The presence of white in a dark fabric will create high contrast. If the contrast within one fabric is significantly greater than the contrast within the other fabrics, it will be difficult to create smooth transitions between fabrics. In this scenario, the best solution would be to eliminate the high-contrast fabric or to add more medium-contrast or high-contrast fabrics to the palette.

High-contrast, multicolored print fabric

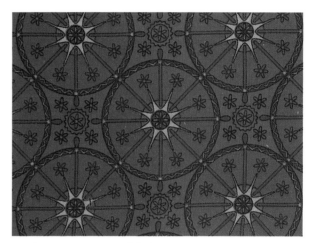

Medium-contrast print fabric

Color and Proportion

Let's say that you have your Big Idea, you have chosen your pattern, and you are standing there in the quilt shop with a stack of bolts in your hand. The pattern calls for a total of four yards of fabric, and you have chosen eight bolts of fabric. Many would just assume that you should get half a yard of each of the fabrics. Note in *diagram 1* how the proportion of color changes the overall feel of the quilt. Refer back to your Big Idea. Are some colors more important than others? Should some colors be used in smaller amounts to lend drama or luminosity to the quilts? Look at the examples in the diagrams for more ideas. For more on color and the Big Idea, read our first book, *Color Harmony for Quilts*.

diagram 1

Now, before you get those fabrics cut, stack them all up on one side of the store and walk to the other side to see how they look. You might not imagine how different some fabrics look up close compared to when viewed across the room. Take the fabrics to a window to check the colors in natural light. The lighting in some quilt shops makes seeing the fabric's true colors difficult.

Design Decisions

Some quilters get so exhausted just choosing the fabrics for the front of the quilt that they leave the quilt shop thinking that they will go back later to choose fabric for the binding and the backing. Whenever possible, try to make those decisions at the same time. This not only saves you a trip to the quilt shop but also ensures that you are going to have everything you need for the quilt. Sometimes the absence of a good backing fabric or a good binding fabric requires that you make changes to the original palette. Moreover, because every design decision you make affects the overall feel of the quilt, you want to consider those choices at the same time that you make the design decisions for the rest of the quilt.

When thinking about the fabric choices for the binding and backing of the quilt, think once again about your Big Idea. For our Gamelan quilt, we wanted the sophisticated circles to dominate the quilt. Had we chose a binding or a backing in anything other than black, it would have

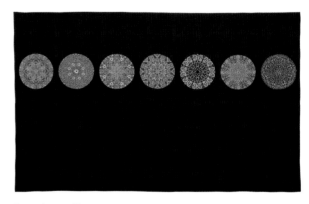

Gamelan quilt

detracted from the fine detail in the circles. In contrast, the Confetti quilt, with its big, chunky pieces, begged to have a smaller-scale, playful binding. Similarly, its brightly colored batiks would have been compromised by anything less than a large-patterned, bright backing fabric.

Confetti quilt

If you are considering a backing fabric that is a totally different color than the colors on the front of the quilt, read the section on choosing thread colors for quilting, page 96, before you buy the fabric. This will ensure that you don't run into problems later choosing thread for quilting.

Audition lots of binding and backing options while you are still in the store. Place the fabrics that you are considering for the binding under the bolts that you are considering for the front. Allow only a 1/2" (0.5 cm) or so to show so you get a true sense of how that fabric would look as a binding. A fabric that looks too bold in an equal amounts on the bolt might add a much-needed bit of zest to a quilt when you are using only 1/2" (0.5 cm) as a binding (*diagram 2*).

Working with Maquettes

Maquette is a French word that describes an artistic prototype. We use it in our teaching because the English translations "mock-up" and "model" have the connotation of lacking detail, and "prototype" sounds too industrial. Maquettes are useful when trying to test color combinations, viewing proportions of color or form, and making general design decisions.

Many quiltmakers are in such a hurry that they want to cut up all of the fabric first and then start laying out the quilt. We recommend that you make a sample block or a small maquette of the quilt before you cut up all of your precious fabric. We have watched many a student cut up yards of a specific green only to realize that it's the wrong green. Making maquettes will help you test all of the design decisions you made at the quilt shop and ensure that you like the finished product. A maquette needs to be only about 20" x 20" (50 x 50 cm) to tell whether it's going to work. Once you have made a few sample blocks, place them on a design wall or layout board and walk across the room to see how they look. We call this the Ten-Foot Rule. For more on the Ten-Foot Rule, please read Design Tips on page 76.

The first swatch seems too bright when seen in equal amounts with the other fabrics, but works well as a slim binding

diagram 2

Making the Quilt

Essential Tools

The Sewing Machine

The sewing machine has transformed the process of making a quilt. If you already have a basic sewing machine that sews reliably and can handle bulky seams, it will most likely be fine for piecing a quilt. If you are in the market for a sewing machine, here are a few features we think are important:

Precision of stitching: All of the quilts in this book require only a straight stitch for piecing. Lower-quality machines sometime slip and slide when sewing through numerous layers of fabric at seams. The rigidity of the needle bar and the power of the motor, plus the quality of the foot, determine whether your machine can sew through multiple layers without slipping. Always test the machine with something very stiff and bulky, such as the outside overlapping seams on a pair of jeans. If the stitching isn't straight, you'll likely have difficulty getting through bulky seams in your quilt.

A walking foot: On most machines, a walking foot is a special foot that replaces the standard presser foot for sewing together several layers of fabric. On some brands, the walking foot is built into the machine. Although some quilters use it only for quilting, we use it for all piecing as well. The walking foot feeds the top layer of fabric at the same rate as the feed dogs advance the bottom layer. A standard foot often drags on the top fabric, causing it to get out of alignment with the bottom layer. In our experience, a walking foot ensures less stretching around curves and precise point alignment. The better brands of sewing machines have a proprietary walking foot that is designed to fit their machines. Inexpensive, generic walking feet rarely work well and are often made of flimsy plastic, which breaks under stress. We always tell students that if it were our money, we would always buy a used machine of a great brand of with a compatible walking foot rather than a newer but lower-quality sewing machine with a generic walking foot.

Features that are nice to have but not essential:

Feed dogs that drop: If you would like to be able to do free-motion quilting, you must have a machine that allows you to drop your feed dogs. Feed dogs are the small teeth under the presser foot that advance the fabric through the machine. Higher-end machines allow you to retract them so you have control over the speed and angle at which the fabric is fed into the machine. Smaller quilts and throws are easy to quilt on a home sewing machine if you can drop your feed dogs.

Needle up/needle down: When you are sewing and need to move your hands or turn a corner, you need to lower the needle into the fabric so the fabric doesn't slip and your stitches don't get out of alignment. You can do this manually by rotating the wheel that controls the needle position. More expensive machines have this feature built into the floor pedal. On our machine, pressing down the heel of your foot makes the

A walking foot is a special foot that replaces the standard presser foot for sewing together several layers of fabric.

needle position go to either the fully up or fully down position. We find this needle up/needle down feature extremely useful.

Presser foot up/down (knee bar): Some machines can be equipped with a knee bar that raises and lowers the presser foot, saving you the strain and repetitive motion of raising and lowering the presser foot by hand.

The Rotary Cutting System

The rotary cutting system includes a rotary cutter, a clear plastic ruler, and a gridded, self-healing cutting mat.

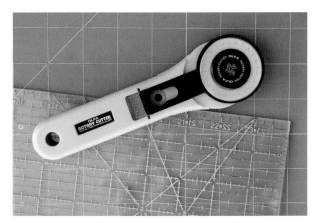

SAFETY WARNING: We cannot overemphasize how sharp these blades are and how important it is to handle rotary cutters with the utmost care. NEVER let a rotary cutter with an exposed blade leave your hand. Get into the habit of closing the blade every time you put it down. If a new rotary blade can slice through eight layers of fabric at a time, imagine the damage it can do if you, a child, or a pet were to bump against it accidentally.

The rotary cutter: The cutter itself works like a pizza cutter but has razor-sharp blades. When you use the rotary cutter in conjunction with the ruler and mat, you can do all of the cutting for your quilt with speed and precision. Several brands and sizes of rotary cutters are on the market. All have replacement blades, and some offer pinking blades as well. The cutters with the largest blades are good for cutting long, straight strips. The smallest cutters are great for cutting curves, "fussy cutting" specific elements in a piece of fabric, and maneuvering around irregularly shaped templates. If you buy only one, buy a medium-size (45 mm) rotary cutter, which gives you a good balance of features. Be aware that cutting paper will dull a rotary blade much faster than cutting fabric, so it's best to assign one blade for cutting fabric and others for cutting paper. We store blades that are too dull for fabric in a case labeled "paper" and use them for paper projects.

The ruler: Several styles of rulers are available. Look for one with easy-to-read numbers and thin, precise measurement lines. Some rulers have the measurements marked in yellow on one side and black on the other so you can read the numbers easily on both dark or light fabrics. Rulers vary in length and width, but a good all-purpose ruler would be 5" (12.5 cm) or 6" (30 cm) wide by 24" (60 cm) long. Some have a lip that helps you maintain a 90° cutting angle against your cutting mat. (Weeks thinks that this is a useful feature, but rulers with lips drive Bill crazy because he thinks that the lip gets in the way if it is not hanging off the edge of the mat.)

Rubber feet for rulers: Some people (such as Weeks and some of our apprentices) think anti-slip feet that adhere to the underside of your ruler are a great idea because they keep the ruler from slipping when you're cutting a long, straight seam. Other people (such as Bill and another apprentice) think they should be outlawed altogether because you can't slide the ruler to make the next cut—you actually have to pick it up. Bill claims that these feet compromise his efficiency. Like many things, it's a matter of choice. Try both and use what is most comfortable for you.

The cutting mat: Self-healing cutting mats let you cut with a rotary cutter over and over without damaging the mat. A mat won't last forever, but you can prolong its life by cutting on it only with a rotary cutter, never a box cutter or utility knife. Mats come in various sizes, from small travel sizes to two-piece mats large enough for cutting tables at quilt shops. Most quilting fabric is 42" (106 cm) wide, so when cutting a large piece of fabric, you will usually fold the fabric to a 21" (53 cm) width, which fits nicely on a 24" x 36" (60 x 90 cm) mat. Having a mat that is a least 24" x 36" (60 x 90 cm) enables you to cut large pieces without worrying about cutting past the edge of the mat (and into your dining room table, perhaps). It also enables you to see all of the measurements easily. Many of our students thought they'd save a little money and buy a smaller mat, but they ended up buying the larger one soon after.

Seam Ripper

You might be amazed at how frequently you need a seam ripper. The little ones that come with some sewing machines are fine for short seams, but for just a few dollars, a more ergonomic one that fits nicely in your hand and has a finer point is priceless when you have a lot of seams to rip out.

Binding Tool (at right)

This tool makes a tiresome chore quick and practically foolproof. It folds your binding fabric perfectly every time. Binding tools are sold in various widths. Using our binding technique as illustrated on page 103, you'll want a 1" (25 mm) binding tool.

Pins/Pincushion

We use long straight pins developed especially for quilting. We like the ones with heat-resistant plastic heads because they are easier to grasp in a hurry and don't melt if they get too close to the iron. The little metal-headed pins you use for sewing clothing are difficult to handle through the thick seams you have to align when making your quilt.

We are indebted to the genius who developed the magnetic pincushion. If you have never used one of these, you don't know how much faster it will make your sewing. Rather than have to place each pin carefully in a pincushion, you can gently toss the pins in the general direction of the magnetic pin cushion, and the magnetic pull keeps them from falling on the ground. Even better, if you drop a pile of pins on the floor, you just wave the pincushion around and they all leap onto it.

Iron

Finding the right iron has been surprisingly difficult. From our experience, you don't always get what you pay for. We went through several expensive "professional" irons, expecting that they would be durable and reliable. Some leaked unpredictably all over our ironing board; others suddenly spewed steam from the sides, burning our hands numerous times. Others just didn't have a good steam output. We finally

Binding tool

settled on a reasonably priced consumer model that cost half the price of the "professional" ones but has proved more reliable and easier to finesse when ironing seams. If you have a good iron with a reliable steam function, keep it. Otherwise, ask your local quilt shop if they have any recommendations. Be aware also that if you drop an iron once, you may have to replace it, so handle it with care. For safety's sake, we prefer irons that shut off after thirty seconds if unused. This also saves electricity, as irons are very high-wattage appliances.

Chalk

Good old dustless schoolboard chalk is a wonderful tool for marking quilts so you don't lose track of your piecing sequence. We favor white or yellow chalk, which washes out easily. Quilt shops sell more expensive disappearing ink pens and chalk pencils for marking quilting patterns, but for remembering the grain of a fabric or differentiating row 1 from row 5 once you're at the sewing machine, nothing beats chalk.

Scissors

You will need scissors mostly to trim threads and trim edges when you're making binding. Try to set aside a good pair of scissors for fabric use only so they don't get dulled by use on paper. You'll be doing almost all of your cutting with the rotary cutter, so an expensive pair of scissors is not necessary.

Template Plastic

Quilt shops sell clear plastic template sheets (some are gridded, some aren't) that are ideal for making cutting templates. For most of the quilts in this book, you can cut all of the pieces just using your rotary system, but a few require templates. Store this material flat and lay out your templates carefully before cutting so you can get the most out of each piece.

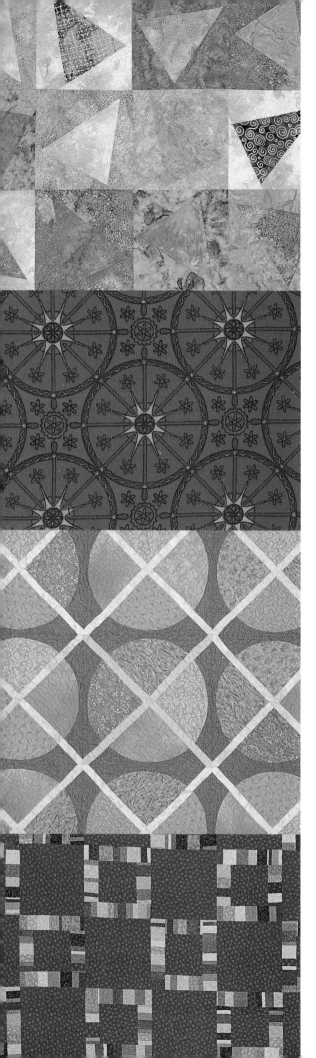

Fabric

If you are making a functional quilt, 100 percent cotton sold at specialty quilt shops is the best fabric to use. Some, but not all, fabric sold at chain fabric shops is lower quality and may shrink unpredictably, bleed onto other fabrics, fade faster, or wear more quickly than the higher-quality cottons found in quilt shops.

Some people want to include fabrics from old clothing in their quilts. The important thing to understand is that the lifespan of the quilt is only as long as the oldest and most worn piece of fabric in it. Weeks once made a Christmas stocking out of antique kimono fabric for a gift. As a Christmas stocking to be used once a year it was fine. For a bed quilt, it would have been a disaster because the antique fabrics would have worn through in a couple of years. Some of our students have used silks to create beautiful wall hangings, but because they can't be washed and dried the way cotton can, they never get the soft, crinkly quality of cotton quilts.

Always prewash your fabrics if you intend to wash the quilt in the future. Over the years we have had even high-quality fabrics bleed. Some fabrics shrink at quicker rates than others. One fabric maker told us that imported fabrics are sometimes manufactured using chemicals that are not considered safe in the United States. You're going to be handling this fabric a lot. Make sure it's clean. Ordinary laundry detergent will hasten the fading of quilting fabrics. A gentle soap or baby shampoo will both clean the fabric and minimize fading.

Thread

Whenever possible, we use 100 percent cotton thread. Polyester thread can melt when the iron is on the cotton setting and also can cut into cotton fabrics over time. Using polyester thread carefully is fine as long as you understand its limitations.

Batting

For all of the quilts we sell, we use 100 percent cotton batting. For charity quilts or for some art quilts, we use a low-loft polyester or polycotton blend. We like 100 percent cotton batting because the shrinking that happens in the dryer with cotton creates a wonderful texture and accentuates our quilting patterns. Polycotton blends and polyester do not shrink, so the quilt will be flat, which some people prefer. Batting is available in several thicknesses called lofts. The poofy, high-loft polyesters can sometimes cause bearding or fiber migration, in which the fibers work their way through the holes in the weave of the fabric and shed outside the quilt for years. We have not had any bearding problems with the low-loft polyesters or blends that resemble felt more than the high-loft fill found in comforters.

Another thing to consider when buying batting is the maximum distance you will be able to have between stitches. Batting manufacturers engineer batting to be stabilized by your quilting stitches. For some types of batting, you will need no expanses greater than 2" to 3" (5–7.5 cm) without quilting stitches, whereas with other types of batting you can go as wide as 6" to 8" (15–20 cm) between stitches. If you exceed the manufacturer's recommendations, the batting may separate within the quilt and become lumpy over time. The packaging will indicate the maximum distance between stitches. If you have any questions about stitch recommendations, ask someone at the quilt shop or contact the manufacturer directly.

Silk and wool batting are less common but are also available at some quilt shops. Read the label on the batting before you use it. Most battings should not be prewashed before use.

Cutting

After you've washed and dried your fabric, iron it. Then match up the selvages (the edges with the manufacturer's name), and look for the natural crease along the fold. Sometimes the store might not have cut straight, and you may have to trim a few inches off to get the fabric to lie flat and the selvages to align somewhat. Don't worry if the selvages don't align perfectly (*diagram 1*).

Align fold on grid

Align edge of ruler on grid of cutting mat and trim to square up fabric

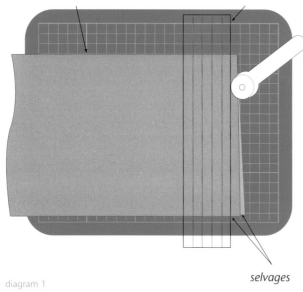

selvages

diagram 1

Make a cut perpendicular to the selvage to get a clean, 90° edge. Follow the cutting instructions for each quilt, avoiding including the selvages in any piece.

Sewing

The standard seam allowance used in quilting is 1/4" (0.5 cm). Before you start sewing, find out where the guideline is on your machine for a 1/4" (0.5 cm) seam. You might need to change your needle position or get another foot to figure it out, but don't start sewing until you are sure that your seam allowance is 1/4" (0.5 cm) (*diagram 2*).

1/4" (0.5 cm) seam allowance

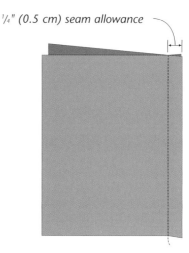

diagram 2

Some of our patterns call for "quick piecing" (also called chain piecing) pairs of pieces or strips. Quick piecing is the process of feeding continuously pairs of pieces through the sewing machine, without stopping to raise the presser foot or cut the thread between pieces. In addition to speeding up the piecing process, quick piecing prevents other problems. Some machines tend to pull the ends of the thread down into the bobbin case, causing the machine to jam. With quick piecing, the sewing is continuous, which reduces jamming. A veteran sewing machine technician told us that the majority of problems with sewing machines happen in the first six stitches of any piece. If the sewing is continuous, there are fewer opportunities for problems with tension, thread ends, or corners of the fabric getting pulled down into the bobbin case.

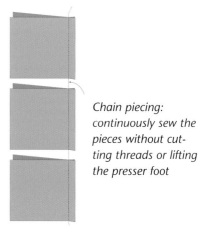

Chain piecing: continuously sew the pieces without cutting threads or lifting the presser foot

diagram 3

Quick piecing is also useful for keeping all of the pieces of a quilt together. Once you have a chain of pieces together, take the whole chain to the ironing board so you don't lose any pieces on the way (*diagram 3*).

In addition to quick piecing, we also use a sewing method we call "leapfrogging." Leapfrogging enables you to sew two rows of a quilt at the same time, further preventing jamming and improving efficiency. Our leapfrogging method also prevents you from mixing up pieces of the quilt when you are moving between the sewing machine, the design wall, and the iron (*see the leapfrogging diagram, page 92*).

Assembling

Once we have cut our pieces, we lay out the quilt on a flannel design wall if it's small enough or, when necessary, on the floor. Flannel is a wonderful friend to quilters because you can stick a piece of quilting cotton to it and it stays put, even on a vertical surface. Some quilters cover a piece of plywood with flannel and use that for laying out their quilts. We use a material called Homosote, which is made from compressed recycled newsprint. Homosote is rigid like plywood yet holds tacks and pins nicely. It comes in 4' x 8' (1.2 x 2.4 m) sheets and is sold at lumberyards. We covered our Homosote with white flannel which enables us to use it as a design wall for piecing by sticking the fabric to the flannel, and also enables us to use it as a space where we can pin up finished quilts, which would be too heavy to adhere to the flannel without pins.

Once you have cut out your pieces, begin to lay them out. Make notes about any fabrics that "pop" or stand out more than you wish. Then observe the Ten-Foot Rule. Fabrics and combinations of fabrics can look different when viewed from two feet (60 cm) away than when viewed from ten feet away (3 m).

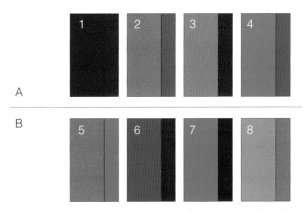

Leapfrog between sewing row A and row B by sewing 1 to 2, then 5 to 6, then 2 to 3, then 6 to 7...

Over and over again, students come to our studio frustrated because they don't think they made good color decisions or their quilt doesn't seem to be coming together the way they thought it would. As soon as we put it up on the design wall and they look at it from ten feet away, the problems with the quilt either no longer seem like problems, or the answers to the problems become clear. Always take a moment to look at your quilt pieces from across the room before you start assembling them—even if you think it looks great. You will see different color adjacencies, and you will have an easier time making design decisions when you can see the whole quilt from a distance.

Once you have finalized the layout of the quilt on the design wall or on the floor, chalk numbers on the pieces so you know the sequencing and can lay them out again should the wind, a pet, or a family member inadvertently rearrange them. Choose a consistent numbering method to prevent yourself from confusing sixes and nines and ones and sevens. We chalk each number in the upper-left corner of the block so we always know its orientation.

This numbering becomes important with directional prints. Some fabrics that do not appear to have any particular direction when you look at them on the bolt suddenly appear to have direction from a distance (yet another reason for the Ten-Foot Rule). You can choose to make sure all of these fabrics face the same direction or not, but what you really don't want is to have is ten of them facing one way and one of them facing the other. Observing the Ten-Foot Rule and developing a consistent chalking strategy will help you avoid this problem.

When you have laid out and chalked all of the pieces, figure out how you can best start leap-frogging (*see the leapfrogging diagram, below*). In the example seen in the numbering diagram on page 91, there are two horizontal rows of four blocks to be sewn. You could take all of the pieces from row A over to the machine, but it would be must faster to alternate, or leapfrog, sewing part of row A with sewing part of row B using the quick-piecing method.

Here's how it would work. Start with row A. Pin blocks 1, 2, 3, and 4 together. For row B, pin blocks 5, 6, 7, and 8 together. Sew block 1 to block 2 in row A. Using the quick-piecing method, do not cut the thread or lift the presser foot—just continue to sew block 5 to block 6 in row B. By this time row A will have cleared the presser foot. Snip the chain that connects the two rows. Now sew blocks 2 and 3 together. Repeat this sequence until both rows are fully pieced.

When all of the rows have been pieced, it's time to iron the seams. The conventional thinking among quilters is that seams should always be ironed to one side. We have tried to speculate how this custom began, because seams are always ironed open when making clothing. We think that this custom originated from the days when people pieced and quilted quilts by hand. Hand stitches are generally larger (4 to 6 stitches per inch [1–3 stitches per cm]) and less durable than stitches from a sewing machine (generally 8 to 12 stitches per inch [3–5 stitches per cm]), and stitching through the seams may

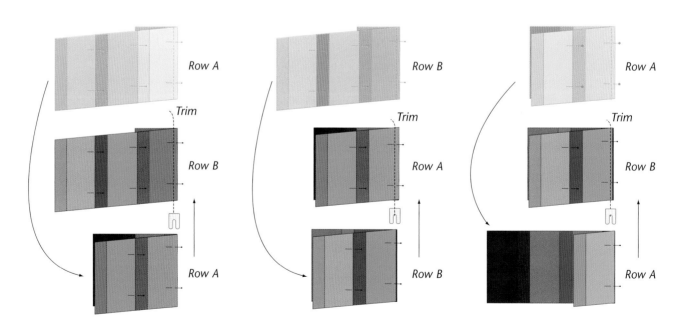

leapfrogging diagram

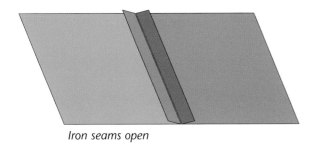

Iron seams open

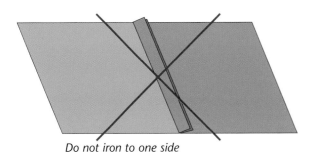

Do not iron to one side

diagram 1

More even quilting: When intersections have seam allowances ironed to one side, they become so bulky that they often have a difficult time clearing the presser foot during the quilting. We always try to quilt through important intersections to minimize bulges at seam intersections and to improve the durability of the quilt. This becomes very difficult, and sometimes impossible, when seams are ironed to one side.

have given the quilt additional reinforcement, which is no longer necessary (*diagram 1*).

So although most quilters we have met have been taught to iron seams to one side, we advise students to iron seams open, unless they plan to piece or quilt by hand. There are a number of reasons that we recommend ironing seams open.

More even wearing: Over time, a bulge will develop on the side of the seam that has three layers of fabric (the fabric and two layers of seam). The bulge will wear faster than it would if there were two layers on each side of the seam.

Improved precision: Some of our designs have intersections where eight points meet. If we were to iron all sixteen seams to one side, the point at which all of the seams meet would become much more bulky and hard to align. Ironing the seams open distributes that bulk and remedies the problem.

Points are easier to match: It is far easier to align points when you can align the seams with pins. Finding the points is much more difficult with the seams sewn to one side.

Piecing Curves

Don't be intimidated by curves. With careful cutting, pinning, and sewing, you'll be able to conquer all the curves in this book. These directions and illustrations work for insetting the half circles in Love Beads as well as for piecing the arcs and quarter circles in the Eclipse quilt and the quarter circles in Gamelan (*diagram 1*).

1. Lay out your quarter circle or half circle and its corresponding piece. Because the curves in this book are large, it is not necessary to notch them.

2. Find the centers of the two pieces by folding them in half. Placing right sides together, align them at the center creases and pin at number 1. Next, pin the edges at numbers 2 and 3. Insert final pins at the midway points, numbers 4 and 5. You can find these midway points by folding the edges to the centers and creasing.

Sew pieces together slowly, keeping the quarter or half circle face-down. If you try to sew it with the circle face-up, you will get puckers. Be careful to maintain a 1/4" (0.5 cm) seam allowance.

3. Iron open the seams on the back then iron the finished piece again on the front.

Inset quarter circle

1. Curves to be pieced

2. Pin curves together and sew

3. Finished block

Inset half circle

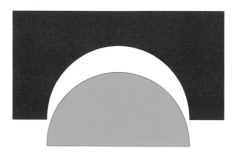

1. Curves to be pieced

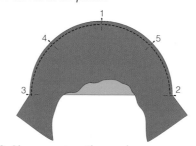

2. Pin curves together and sew

3. Finished block

diagram 1

Pinning

When you have pieced all of the pieces in each row, it is time to piece the rows together. This is when it becomes important to align points. The best way to ensure that points are going to align is to cut and pin carefully.

With row A in your hand, stick a pin through the point that is in the seam between piece 1 and piece 2 and 1/4" (2.5 cm) from the raw edge. Find that same point on row B and stick the pin through it as well (*diagram 2*). Secure the pin perpendicular to the seam you will be sewing. If you are sewing a long row of blocks, continue pinning until all of the intersections in the row have been aligned. If the intersections are slightly off, try to stretch the fabrics enough that you won't get any tucks when you sew the rows together.

Remove the pin just before it disappears under the presser foot. Although we have heard many people say they just sew right over pins, we have inadvertently sewn over pins many times and have either broken or irreparably bent needles. On a few occasions, the part of the needle that has broken off has flown onto our faces or into our eyes. Be safe. Pull the pins out before they become a danger.

1/4" (0.5 cm)

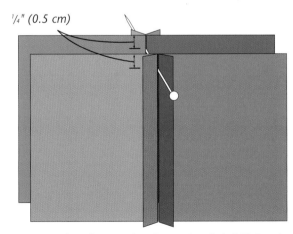

Pinning right sides together, insert the pin 1/4" (0.5 cm) from the edge and in between the seams of both pieces

diagram 2

When you have pieced the entire top of the quilt, iron open all of the seams and turn it over so you can iron it from the front as well. The flatter the quilt, the easier it will be to quilt.

Quilting

Quilting as a Design Layer

By the time a quilt is ready to be quilted, some students are anxious to finish the project. We encourage students to take some time to revisit their Big Idea and think about the quilting pattern and thread color as yet another design layer to the quilt. Often a uniform quilting pattern that unites different parts of the quilt is successful, whereas sometimes quilting patterns that contrast with different parts of a quilt can be complementary.

If you plan to wash and dry your quilt, think of the texture that a given quilting pattern is going to impart on the quilt. This is a great time to consider doing a few maquettes so you can see a few quilting samples before you commit to doing the whole quilt. Make a few extra blocks and audition some thread colors and patterns. Wash and dry the maquettes and see how the different patterns and colors will change the overall feel of the quilt. If you're confused about which batting to select, this is also a good chance to quilt with different types of batting. Ask quilting friends, manufacturers, or quilt shops if they have any samples. Our favorite manufacturer of batting gives us 12" x 12" (30 cm x 30 cm) squares of cotton batting to give students to try.

Stay out of the Ditch!

The wrong thread color or pattern can ruin an otherwise beautiful quilt. Most experienced quilters know this. Others opt for quilting in the seams created by the piecing, also known as "stitching in the ditch" (*diagram 3*). There are so many problems created by stitching in the

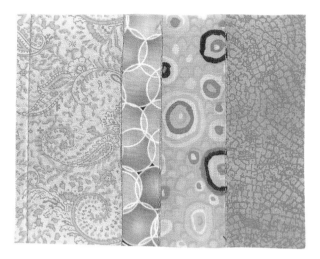

Stitching in the ditch often ends up looking sloppy

diagram 3

ditch that we would not be disappointed if this practice fell out of favor all together.

Stitching in the ditch can compromise the durability of a quilt. In some quilts we have seen, the needle of the machine has gone straight through the thread that is holding the pieces together, weakening the seam irreparably. In others, the quilting has wandered in and out of the ditch, making an otherwise nicely crafted quilt look really sloppy. Finally, stitching in the ditch adds no beauty to a quilt. It may hold a quilt together, but the whole point of stitching in the ditch is to disguise the quilting. If you've done a nice job with the quilting, it improves the quilt. Rather than putting the energy into hiding the stitching, we think you should always think about how the stitching can improve the quilt.

Tying: A Cautionary Tale

We have seen many beautiful quilts that have been tied instead of quilted. In tying, the quilter uses ribbons, thread, yarn, or embroidery floss to attach the three layers of the quilt. Rather than uniform stitching across the entire quilt, ties are often located at the corners of blocks or every 4" to 6" (5–7.5 cm). If you do not intend to wash the quilt, this solution might work fine. If, however, you plan to give the quilt to someone else or you intend to wash it, tying is not a good solution.

We recently were asked by a despondent eight-year-old boy to fix his beloved "blankie." The much-used quilt had been tied with yarn and filled with poofy polyester batting. At the location of the ties, large holes had developed through years of cuddling and washing. The batting was falling out through the holes created by the ties, and it was so thin that you could see through it.

Taking pity on this child and the quilt's maker, who had made this quilt with wonderful intentions, we tried to figure out how we could save what was left of the quilt. We determined that the only way to save it was to take out all of the ties and take the quilt apart. We decided to laminate the navy blue backing fabric with the worst holes in it to another piece of fabric to prevent the new batting from falling through the holes. Using a temporary basting spray, we placed the navy blue print on top of another piece of navy blue fabric. Then we reassembled the quilt, this time with cotton batting. Using our long-arm quilting machine, we densely quilted the entire piece, paying special attention to the areas around the holes so they would remain attached to the new fabric.

There are many morals to this story—most important is that a quilt given to a child at birth sometimes becomes his or her most cherished possession. Tying might be fine for wall hangings or holiday decorations but is not a good choice for children's quilts. Quilts given to children should be of the highest durability, for they will be washed frequently, and children will use them for all sorts of things unrelated to sleeping. As every child knows, a quilt is the best cape for any superhero and the best tablecloth for any tea party.

diagram 1

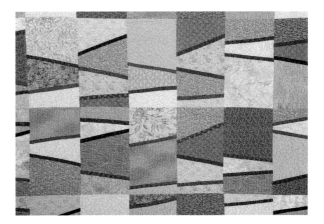

diagram 2

Choosing Thread for Quilting

Here are a few guidelines for choosing thread colors for quilting. Revisit your Big Idea. Try to focus on what role you want the quilting to have. For example, in Unfinished Business (page 74), we used five colors of thread to echo the color shifts seen in the quilt. The thread colors were selected to reinforce the color work in the piecing. If we had used the same thread color across the whole quilt, it would have distracted from the color shifts.

In contrast, we chose to use one thread color and an overall quilting pattern for the Marquee quilt (page 34). The overall meandering pattern, known among quilters as "stippling" or "vermicelli," was designed to provide an overall subtle texture to the quilt. We felt that the contrast between the marquee strips and the red background was strong enough that a complex quilting pattern or highly contrasting thread would make the quilt too busy.

When choosing a thread color, look at the darkest or most intense color in the quilt and then the lightest color in the quilt. Sometimes the best thread color, if you are going to use only one, is the color that is halfway between the two extremes found in the quilt. Sometimes it is not even a color seen in the quilt. Imagine how much spunk a red thread would add to a black and white quilt.

Many quilters feel as though the thread must match all of the parts of the quilt, so they use variegated thread to lessen the contrast between the thread and the piecing. Although this method might work some of the time, with busier quilts it might become too much. Another way to think about thread choices—and quilting patterns, for that matter—is to think about whether you want the quilting to "turn up the volume" of the quilt or to "turn it down." In Plain Spoken, the thread color and the quilting pattern turn down the volume by uniting the different colored rectangles. In Gamelan, the thread colors help differentiate the kaleidoscopic circles from the black background. In Boomerang, the thread colors and the quilting patterns reinforce the different forms (*diagram 1*). Look closely at the detail of Treehouse (*diagram 2*). Notice that we have left the brown "branches" unquilted to accentuate them.

Another factor to consider when choosing thread colors is how the thread will look on the backing fabric. Although it is true that you can use different colors of thread on the front and back of the quilt, we have found that if the thread colors are very different in value (the lightness or darkness of the color), the contrasting thread can sometimes be visible on the other side. For example, if you were to use black thread on one side of a quilt and white thread on the other, you might see black dots along the quilting lines that might not be what you had in mind. A maquette will help you determine whether different threads for the front and back of the quilt will pose a problem for you. Minimizing the value differences between the thread color on the front and that on the back will greatly simplify your thread color dilemmas.

Confused even further about choosing a thread colors, some opt for using clear plastic thread or "monofilament," which looks like a thin version of fishing line. With a little bit of thought, anyone should be able to choose a good thread color with confidence. The best reason to avoid quilting with monofilament, however, is the way it makes your quilt feel. If you have ever worn a garment with a prickly tag, you know how sharp monofilament thread can be against the skin. Should a thread break on a quilt quilted with monofilament, you will forever have that itchy-thread feel in your quilt.

Preparing to Quilt

There are many wonderful aspects of hand-quilting, the greatest of which is the portability of it. We know one quilting teacher who makes all of her quilts entirely by hand as her retired husband drives their RV all over the country.

Other "spectator sports widows" embrace hand-quilting as a way to sit in a room during a football game but to do something that holds their interest more than the game. If you are interested in learning to quilt by hand, Jinny Beyer's book *Quiltmaking by Hand* is one of the most comprehensive books on the subject. For more information, see the Resources section of this book.

Although traditionalists may feel that hand-quilting is preferable to machine-quilting, we prefer machine-quilting for its durability and the texture you can achieve by stitching far more densely than would be possible with hand-

quilting. Nearly all of the students we have had also prefer machine-quilting to hand-quilting. With years of hand-quilting, you need to be careful of developing carpal tunnel syndrome or arthritis. The main reason people prefer machine-quilting over hand-quilting, however, is time. Using a long-arm quilting machine, we can quilt a twin-size quilt in two to three hours, and on a home machine it might take only a weekend, whereas hand-quilting could easily take more than 100 hours.

As you think about machine-quilting, try to design a pattern that includes a continuous line. Sometimes a design does not permit this, but it is always better to be able to hide the ends of the threads under the binding than it is to have them visible throughout the front of the quilt. Invariably you will end up with some loose ends exposed because your bobbin will run out in the middle of the quilt. But if the design has a lot of starting and stopping, the quilt will wear much more quickly, and the loose ends will work their way loose and look ragged faster than you'd like. If your quilting design calls for lots of stopping and starting, decrease the stitch length at the beginning and end of each segment so the quilting doesn't work its way loose any sooner than necessary.

So, let's review some options.

Straight stitching on your home machine: Even the simplest, oldest sewing machine can handle straight stitching a quilt if it's not too large, if you have set up your workspace well, and if you prepare your quilt carefully.

Free-motion stitching on your home machine: You can try free-motion quilting on your home machine if you are able to drop the feed dogs. In free-motion quilting, the feed dogs do not advance the quilt through the machine. The speed at which you push the fabric through the machine in conjunction with the amount of pressure you are placing on the pedal foot

Adventures in Long-Arm Quilting

In June 1999, we bought our long-arm quilting machine. We were thrilled at the prospect of being able to quilt a queen-size bed quilt in a day and were ecstatic at the prospect of never having to baste again! The only person we knew with a long-arm machine was the sales rep, and we had no idea what we were in for.

It took us a good month and several ruined quilts to realize that the sales rep had taught us to thread the machine incorrectly and installed the wrong needles for the type of batting that we were using. With this 14' (4.25 m) machine that consistently had threading and tension problems, we became more than a little disillusioned. With Bill's natural mechanical skills, several trips to the needle supply shop, numerous calls to the manufacturer, and hours of tinkering, we finally got the machine to quilt. Once we got it working, we loved it, but we always advise people who are considering buying a long-arm machine to plan on becoming a mechanic and detective too, because there is no long-arm machine repair guy in the phone book.

The advantage of the long-arm machine is that all the layers of the quilt are stretched tautly throughout the entire quilting process. Rather than move the quilt through the machine as you would in free-motion quilting, you move the sewing head around the quilt. This eliminates the dreaded basting process, and means that the quilt stays square and that you can work much more quickly.

We rent time on our machine and know of a few other places around the country that do as well. We have listed some organizations of long-arm quilters in the Resources section. Call a few near you and ask whether they rent time on their machines. Most require a training class of some type, but once you have mastered the basics, you are set to go. Many quilt shops will finish your quilt for you on their machine for a fee but will not rent it out to you. We always discourage students from hiring other people to finish their quilts, because the quilting and binding is such an important part of the quilt, and quilt finishers can sometimes have a "one style fits all" approach to quilting and binding quilts. The Big Idea as it relates to the quilting and binding is often lost on someone who doesn't share or understand the inspiration for the quilt.

There are, however, communities in which renting time on a long-arm quilting machine is not an option, and it's not practical to finish a large quilt on your home machine. We have had more than a few people who live in other parts of the country include renting time on our long-arm as part of a visit to Chicago. If there are no rental places in your area, check availability in other cities you visit. If renting is an option, please give it a try before you turn over your next quilt to someone else. A good rental place will provide you with training and let you try a few patterns on muslin or scrap fabric before you commit to starting your quilt.

We do not finish other people's quilts but are willing to provide them with the skills to finish it themselves. As a result, we have had dozens and dozens of students who, had we been willing to do it for them, would never have learned to finish their own quilts. Some students have told us that they were afraid of the machine because it is so big. They have said that they were afraid they would break the machine or ruin their quilt if they tried to do it themselves. Many felt a tremendous surge in confidence that they not only had mastered a new skill by learning how to operate the machine but also became much more creative in their approach to the quilting process. A few have told us that they get so excited about renting the machine that they wake up the morning of their rental and look forward to it all day. We know of only one person who tried a long-arm machine and did not enjoy it. If you have the opportunity to learn how to quilt using a long-arm quilting machine, you owe it to yourself to try.

determines how long and how consistent your stitches will be. If you have never done free-motion quilting before, make a few maquettes before you start on your quilt.

Basting

If you plan to quilt your quilt on a home sewing machine or by hand, you will need to baste together all of the layers. Quilt shops are filled with tools and gizmos to simplify the basting process, because it is one of the least enjoyable aspects of quilting. The goal of basting is to attach temporarily the backing fabric, the batting, and the front of the quilt so the whole piece remains flat during the quilting process. If you don't baste the layers, you risk the top slipping from the batting and backing, the corners of the quilt not remaining square, and tucks developing in the batting or backing. However dreary and time-consuming this step may be, you risk disaster by skipping it if you plan to quilt on a standard sewing machine or by hand.

Decide which method of basting is the most manageable for you. Some people use hundreds of grooved safety pins. Other prefer a needle and thread. We have also seen people invest in a system that looks like the gizmos that attach price tags to clothing, which shoot plastic strings through all of the layers of the quilt. Still others use a temporary spray adhesive. There is even fusible, iron-on batting available. Regardless of the method you choose, follow these basic guidelines to make basting as fast and successful as possible.

The first step in basting is to find a large, flat surface on which to lay all of the layers of the quilt. If you plan to use a dining room table or any surface that might get nicked by a needle, be sure to protect it with mats or towels. If you plan to baste on carpeting, take care not to pick up some of the carpet fibers while you baste. We have heard more than a few stories of people who inadvertently basted their quilt to their carpets.

Plan on a time and place where children and pets will not be running across your project. Then lay out your backing piece with the wrong side up. Make sure that your backing fabric is at least 2" (5 cm) longer on all sides than the front of your quilt. Check to make sure that all of the seams have been ironed flat and that there are no wrinkles on the backing.

Now carefully position the batting on top of the backing, making sure that it too is at least 2" (5 cm) longer on all sides than the front of the quilt. Beginning in the center of the quilt, smooth out the batting until there are no wrinkles in it. Check that in the smoothing process you have not created wrinkles in the backing. Now carefully position the quilt top in the center of the batting, ensuring that it is totally flat and that you have at 2" (5 cm) of batting and backing on all sides.

Once the "sandwich" is totally flat and without wrinkles, start basting. If you are using a special basting system, follow the manufacturer's recommendation on spacing. If you are using a needle and thread or safety pins, lightly chalk a 4" (10 cm) grid onto the quilt. If you are using safety pins, pin the intersections of the grid, starting in the middle of the quilt and making sure that the quilt stays flat as you go. If you are using a needle and thread, start in the center of the quilt. Choose a thread color that is easy to see against the quilt to make it easier to remove later. Thread the needle with a very long (50" to 60" [125–150 cm]) single strand of thread. Do not make a knot at either end of the thread. Make one stitch in the center of quilt, then pull the needle off of the thread and pull the ends until they meet. Place one end on the quilt and rethread the needle with the other end. Start basting along the grid in continuous, long, 2" to 3" (5–7.5 cm) stitches. Continue basting until you run out of thread. Then remove the needle and rethread it with the other end of the thread. Now baste in the other direction until the thread runs out. Continue this process until the whole quilt is basted. The advantage to this long-thread technique is that you will have the longest possible thread in your basting, which will make it easier to remove after you've finished the quilting.

Chalking or Taping Patterns

Quilt shops offer hundreds of quilting pattern templates, disappearing pens, and chalk pencils, which some people use to mark quilts in preparation for quilting. We have always chosen to quilt our quilts using freehand quilting or by chalking simple lines or circles as guidelines. Tracing around the edges of mixing bowls or plates is a free way of chalking circle guidelines. Look around your house for other objects you might be able to trace to create guidelines for a new quilting pattern. Also try freehanding a few patterns on some muslin or scrap fabric.

A useful method for marking straight lines is to use painter's tape. Painter's tape has low tackiness and can be repositioned on fabric over and over. Simply place the tape on the area of the quilt you intend to quilt. By aligning the edge of your presser foot with the edge of the tape, you can sew a perfectly straight line with no marking. If you want your lines to be 2" (5 cm) apart, for example, you can buy a 2" (5 cm)-wide roll of tape and use the opposite edge of the tape for your next line. Then you can move the tape, aligning one edge with the straight line you just sewed and sewing the new line along the other edge of the tape.

Before you place any tape on your quilt, test it on a scrap of fabric to make sure it does not leave behind any adhesive. The adhesives on some tapes deteriorate over time, so use a new

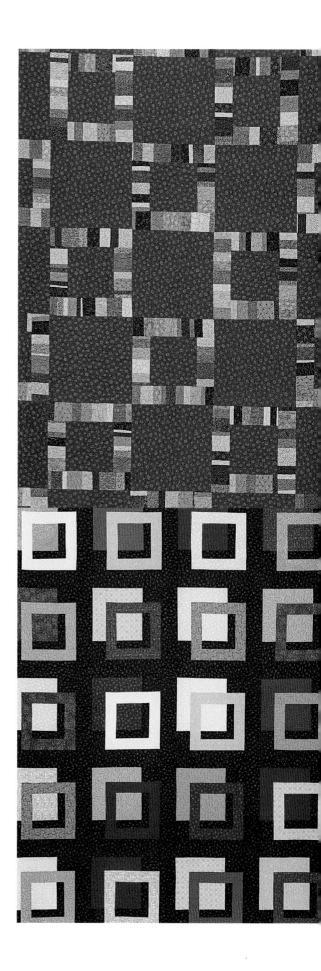

roll of tape if possible. In addition, to minimize any residual adhesive, do not allow tape to remain in the same place on the quilt for more than 24 hours.

Fitting the Quilt into the Machine

Once you have basted and marked your quilt, you are ready to quilt. It's always a good idea to start the quilting in the center of the quilt so you can smooth out any wrinkles or tucks before they get sewn. If your quilt is rectangular, you will want to start rolling it along the longest sides to minimize the bulk that has to fit in the throat of the sewing machine. Roll from one side toward the center, and then roll from the other side until the area that you want to quilt is all that is exposed. You will probably want to quilt an area about 24" (60 cm) wide at a time, depending on the design. Some quilters find giant clamps sold at quilt shops helpful in stabilizing the quilt once it's rolled up. Others use safety pins to keep it from unrolling.

When you are ready to start quilting, set up a space on the other side of your machine and some sort of support behind you to catch the quilt as you work on the opposite end. Most quilters find it easiest to throw the quilt roll over their shoulder to make it easier to feed the quilt through the machine. If your piece is very long, an ironing board or table behind you will ease the weight of the quilt on your shoulders and help keep your stitching as smooth as possible. Each time you move the quilt through the machine, make sure that the backing is still flat.

When you need a break or are ready to reposition the quilt, put the needle in the down position if you are in the middle of a line of quilting. This will prevent the threads from being pulled out of alignment and making your quilting look sloppy. Ideally, finish the quilting all the way to the edge so you don't have to worry. But the reality is that phones ring, and sometimes you just have to stop in the middle of the quilt.

When free-motion quilting, you should aim for a stitch length of 8 to 12 stitches per inch (3–5 stitches per cm). If your stitches are longer than that, either increase the pedal speed or move the quilt around more slowly. If your stitches are shorter than that, decrease the pedal pressure. With free-motion quilting, moving a bulky quilt around more quickly to increase your stitch length is easier said than done.

Binding

The binding is that piece of fabric that covers the raw edge of the quilt. Although its role in a quilt is primarily functional, you should not underestimate how much a great binding can enhance a quilt. Conversely, an uninspired binding is a missed opportunity. Remember the Modernist architect Mies van der Rohe's proclamation that "God is in the details."

Every quilting book we have ever seen suggests that the binding must be made from strips cut on a bias (*diagram 1*). The bias refers to the angle that is 45° from the selvage of the fabric. The theory goes that cutting through the grain

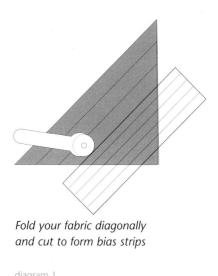

*Fold your fabric diagonally
and cut to form bias strips*

diagram 1

of the fabric will make the binding lie flatter. Having a bias-cut binding is critical if the edges of your quilt are not straight, if they are scalloped, or if the corners are rounded. If the edges of your quilt are straight and your corners are squared, a bias-cut binding is not critical.

In fact, we hardly ever use bias-cut bindings and instead opt for bindings made from strips cut on the grain. The most obvious benefit to on-grain bindings is that they are far less wasteful of fabric and far faster to make than those that are cut on the bias. We love the crinkly

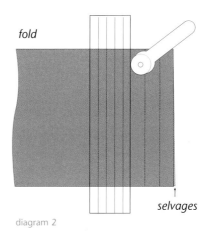

fold

selvages

diagram 2

texture of our quilts, so the argument that you should use a bias binding so the binding lies flat does not resonate with us. When cutting on-grain binding strips, cut all of the strips from selvage to selvage (*diagram 2*).

Another issue of concern to many quilters is how to attach the binding to the quilt. Most quilters use a technique in which they break down the sewing into two steps—one that is sewn by machine and one that is sewn by hand. Unless there is some compelling design reason to the contrary, we opt for a one-step machine-sewn binding. We think that this technique is not only faster but also appropriate to our modernist aesthetic. Some students have told us that it has taken them a few tries to master but that in the end it is worth it. The traditional method uses 3" (7.5 cm) strips, whereas the one-step method uses 2" (5 cm) strips.

We will show you both methods of binding, and you can decide which is appropriate for your quilt.

In both the traditional and one-step binding methods, you will need to make a strip of fabric that is a few inches longer than the perimeter of the quilt. Calculate the perimeter of the quilt by measuring the length of all sides and adding the measurements together. For example, if you are making a 30" x 40" (76 x 102 cm) baby quilt, the perimeter of your quilt is 140" (356 cm).

For both techniques, the method for piecing together the binding is the same (*see diagram 1 for general instructions*).

Place the ends of two 2" (5 cm)-wide strips, right sides together, so they form an L.

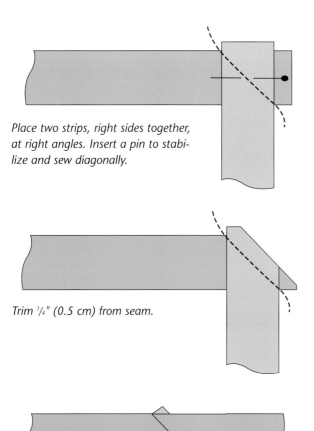

Place two strips, right sides together, at right angles. Insert a pin to stabilize and sew diagonally.

Trim ¹/₄" (0.5 cm) from seam.

Iron seams open.

diagram 1

1. Sew across the diagonal line seen in the diagram. You will be sewing the pieces together at a 45° angle, without chalking or measuring.

2. Using the quick piecing method, continue sewing the other pieces together until all of the strips are done.

   Note: If you are using solid fabrics or batiks in which there is no apparent right side, decide on a right side and mark both of the ends of each strip with a small chalk mark. This will prevent you from inadvertently mixing up right sides and wrong sides in the same strip.

3. Trim with scissors approximately ¹/₄" (0.5 cm) from the seam.

4. Iron open all of the seams. By sewing the seams at an angle, you will distribute the bulk along a greater distance.

If you want make a pieced binding, such as the one in the Confetti quilt on page 42, you will not be piecing at a 45° angle but rather at a standard 90° angle. Your seams will be bulky, but the aesthetics make it worth the bulkiness for a special binding.

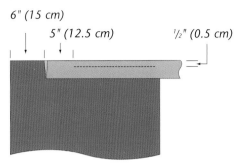

Piece 3" (8 cm) binding strips the length of the quilt perimeter plus a little extra. Fold strip in half and iron.

6" (15 cm)

5" (12.5 cm)   ½" (0.5 cm)

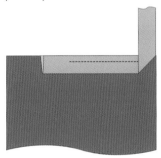

Place ironed strip along raw edge of top side of the quilt 6" (15 cm) from corner. Begin sewing 5" (12.5 cm) from end of bingin strip so you can later splice the ends together. Sew ½" (0.5 cm) from the edge of quilt and stop ½" (0.5 cm) from the corner.

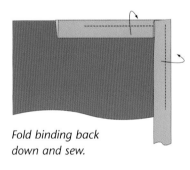

Fold binding up.

Fold binding back down and sew.

Fold binding over to back side of quilt and form miters. Follow directions for the splicing ends together then blind stitch binding by hand on the front to finish.

diagram 2

Traditional Binding

The traditional binding technique is done in two steps. The first step is attaching the binding to the front of the quilt, which is done by machine.

1. Iron your 3" (7.5 cm)-wide binding strip in half lengthwise, right side out, aligning the raw edges carefully as you go.

2. Align the raw edge of the quilt with the raw edge of your binding.

3. Start sewing 5" (12.5 cm) down from the end of the strip and about 6" (15 cm) from one of the corners of the quilt. Leave the end loose so you can splice it to the other end of the binding strip when you're done.

4. Miter the corners by folding the edges as shown.

5. Sew the binding all the way around the quilt, taking care to miter each corner carefully.

6. When you have mitered the last corner, lay the binding strip along the edge of the quilt until it overlaps with the starting end of the binding strip. Cut the end so both strips overlap by ½" (1 cm). This will allow you to splice together the ends with ¼" (0.5 cm) seam allowances for both ends.

7. Splice together the ends as shown and sew the final section of the binding to the quilt.

8. Now turn the quilt over, wrapping the ironed edge of the binding around the back of the quilt.

9. Pin the binding to the quilt, taking special care to miter the corners.

10. Using a needle and a doubled strand of thread, sew the edge of the binding to the back of the quilt using a blind stitch.

One-Step Binding

Making the Binding (*diagram 1*)

1. Using a 1" (2.5 cm) binding, feed the end of the strip into the binding tool.

2. As you pull the fabric through the binding tool, you will see that the raw edges of the fabric meet in the middle of the strip.

3. Iron the binding flat as it comes through the binding tool, making sure that the raw edges remain in the center of the strip.

4. When you have worked the whole strip through the binding tool, align the ironed edges by folding the strip in half lengthwise.

5. Iron the whole strip until the binding strip is flat.

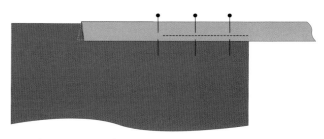

Snugly wrap ironed binding around raw edge of quilt.

Place strip 6" (15 cm) from corner and begin sewing about 5" (12.5 cm) from end of binding strip so you can later splice the ends together. Sew ⅛" (0.25 cm) from edge of binding.

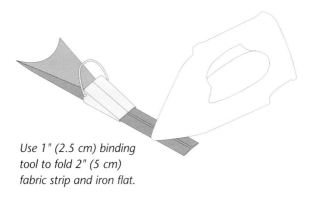

Use 1" (2.5 cm) binding tool to fold 2" (5 cm) fabric strip and iron flat.

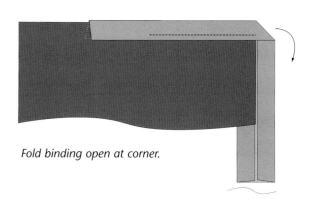

Fold binding open at corner.

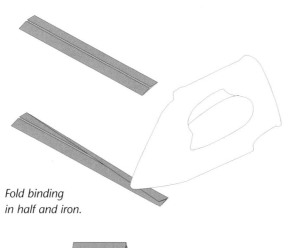

Fold binding in half and iron.

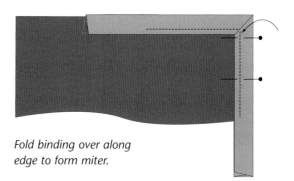

Fold binding over along edge to form miter.

diagram 1   diagram 2

Attaching the Binding (*diagram 2*)

1. Starting 6" (15 cm) down from one corner of the quilt and leaving a loose end of 5" (12.5 cm), wrap the binding around the raw edge of the quilt and pin. It should fit snugly and evenly.

2. Using your left hand to guide the quilt under the presser foot and your right hand to make sure the binding does not separate from the quilt, sew a seam $1/8$" (0.25 cm) from the inner edge of the binding.

3. Keep sewing the binding all the way to the edge of the quilt.

4. Lift the presser foot and cut the thread.

5. Holding the quilt in your left hand, place your right thumb in the inside of the binding strip along the raw edges.

6. As you pull the strip down to turn the corner, you will see that a 45° miter has formed on the front. Fold the same miter the same way and sew it flat using a reverse stitch to tack the ends of the threads.

7. Continue sewing until you have mitered the last corner. As you turn the corner, wrap the binding around the raw edge until it overlaps with the end of the loose starting strip.

8. Cut the end of the strip $1/2$" (1 cm) longer than the overlap so you can splice the strips together and maintain a $1/4$" (0.5 cm) seam allowance (*diagram 3*).

9. Open both ends of the ironed binding strip, and splice them together.

10. Refold the binding and wrap it around the edge of the quilt. It should fit snugly.

11. Bind the last section of the quilt.

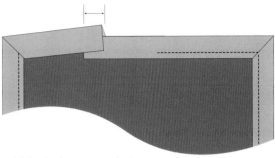

Fold final edge over and trim binding so the beginning and end overlap by $1/2$" (1.25 cm)

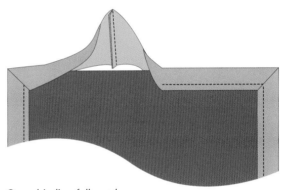

Open binding fully and sew ends together with a $1/4$" (0.5 cm) seam allowance.

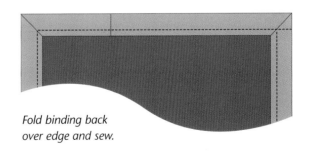

Fold binding back over edge and sew.

diagram 3

Caring for Quilts

A wealth of information on the care of quilts is available on the Internet and at your local library. We recommend all quilters read *From Fiber to Fabric*, by Harriet Hargraves, the seminal book on the care of cotton fabric and quilts. The advice Hargraves gives is well researched and appropriate for quilts that are keepsakes, wall hangings, or other pieces not meant to be used frequently.

We have found that there are two principal schools of thought about the use of quilts. Some prefer to keep their quilts for display purposes only, keeping them carefully folded in closets, away from light, and beyond the reach of anyone's hands but their own. If you are one of these people, you should follow Hargraves's advice, handwashing your quilts in special equine shampoo sold at quilt shops and air-drying them on two clotheslines or flat on the grass in your yard.

Although we feel that this method is appropriate for antique or show quilts, it is not practical for people who want to use their quilts daily or those who don't have yards for air-drying, or for those times in the middle of winter when the quilt just needs to be washed. Some people feel that quilts are meant to be used in accordance with life in the twenty-first century. They should be placed throughout the house, used by children as objects of play and by pets as inviting surfaces on which to nap. These people believe in washing and drying their quilts by machine, and if the quilts fade over time, they will make more.

If you can follow Hargraves's advice, do so. We tend to live with many of the quilts we have made and thus fall into the latter school of thought. We have a front-loading washing machine, which is far more gentle on textiles and vastly more efficient in energy and water use than top-loading models. A cap of baby shampoo in a cold wash is far more gentle, according to Hargraves's research, than soaps marketed for delicates and hand-washables. Although Hargraves warns against it, we do machine-dry our quilts, because we love the texture and softness it produces. Given that in some months we wash more than a dozen quilts, air-drying is not practical for our urban lifestyle in a cold region like Chicago. For the antique quilts we own, we follow Hargraves's recommendations.

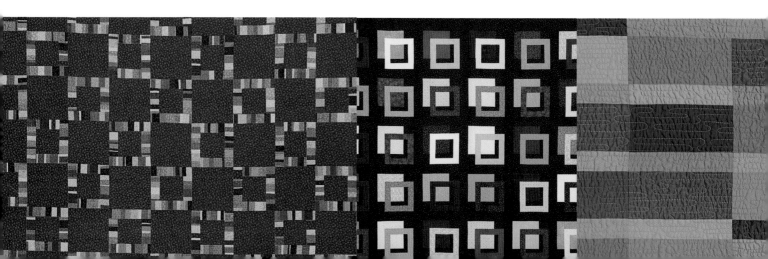

One aspect of quilt care that nearly everyone agrees upon is that dry cleaning compromises the long-term structure of the fibers and should be avoided.

Once you have washed and dried your quilt, if you want to store it in a closet, fold it carefully in an old sheet or a large piece of muslin. Textile conservators discourage us from storing quilts in plastic bags or boxes for long periods of time, because the fibers need to breathe. We store many of our quilts in large plastic bins because we take them out at least once a month for teaching or showing to clients. Whenever we take them out, we fold them differently when we put them away so that the creases created by the folds will not become permanent. Folding them in thirds sometimes, in half other times, and in seemingly random patterns other times helps maintain the long-term structure of the quilt.

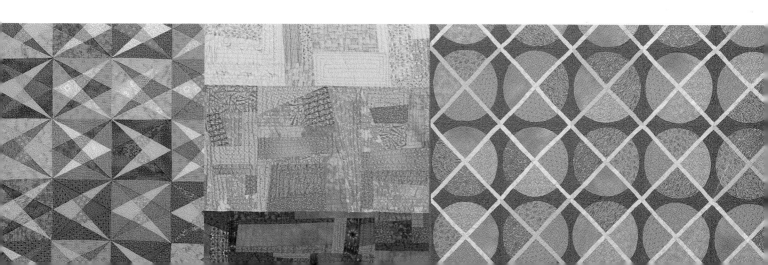

Appendix

Templates

To copy templates onto template plastic, place your plastic over the pattern and trace with a pen that does not smear on plastic, such as a permanent fine-tipped pen. The solid lines are the edges of the templates. The dashed lines indicate the finished seams. The alternating dash-dot-dash lines are for alignment later. The crossed arrows indicate the direction of the fabric grain when important. Trace all of these lines onto your template plastic, label the template part, and cut out along the solid lines. We keep templates for each project organized in labeled envelopes.

We place a loop of clear tape on the back of each template to prevent it from slipping when cutting fabric.

Eclipse template B

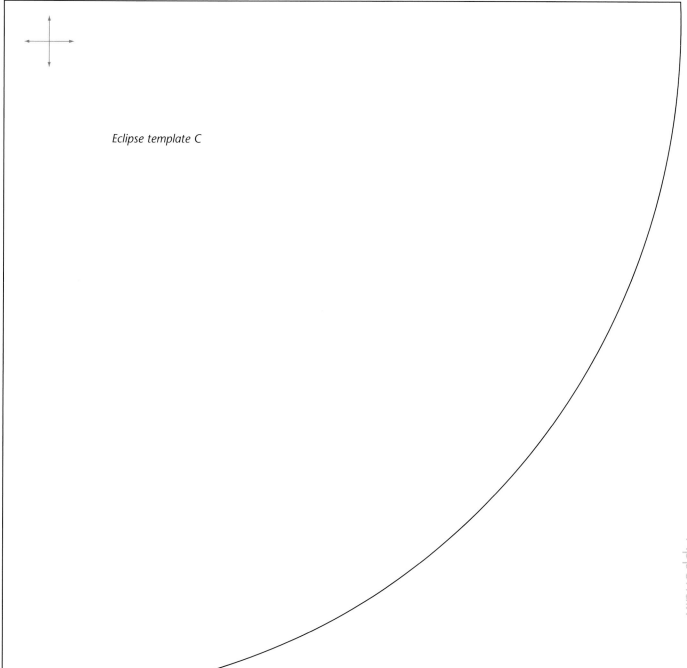

Eclipse template C

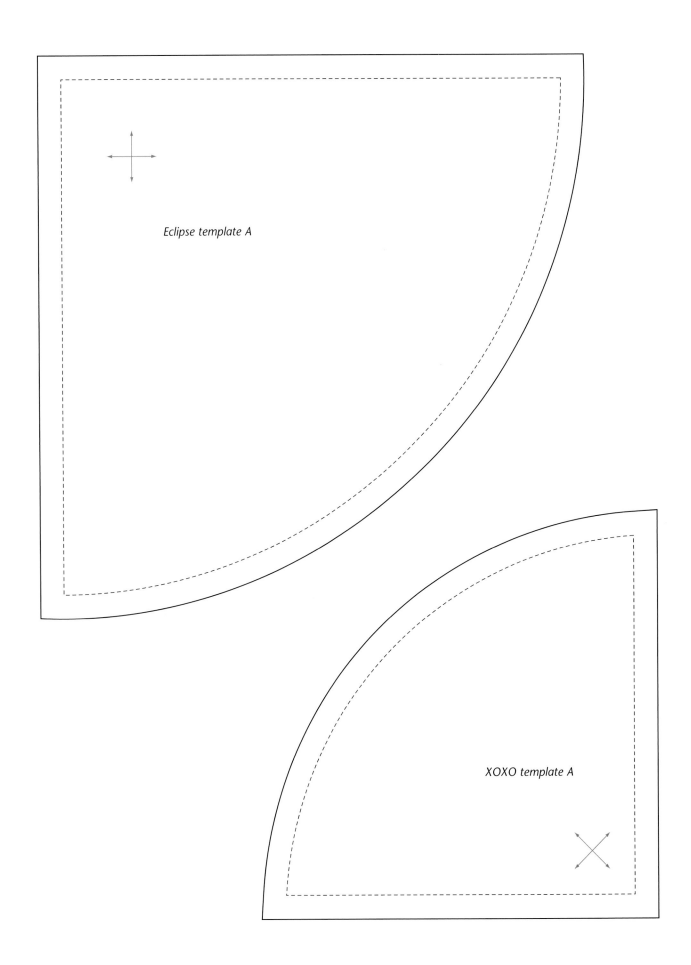

Eclipse template A

XOXO template A

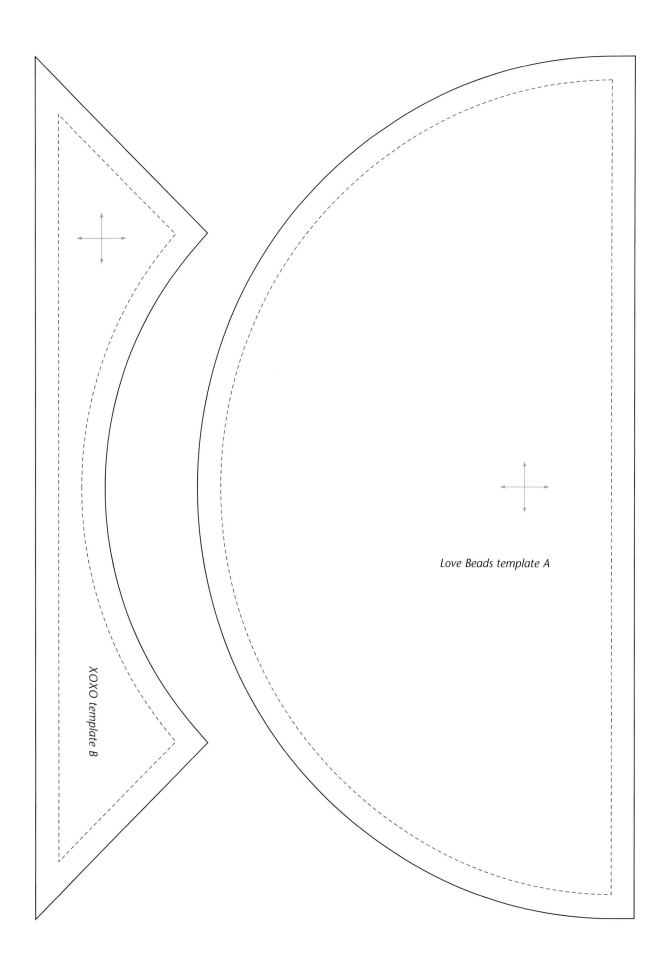

XOXO template B

Love Beads template A

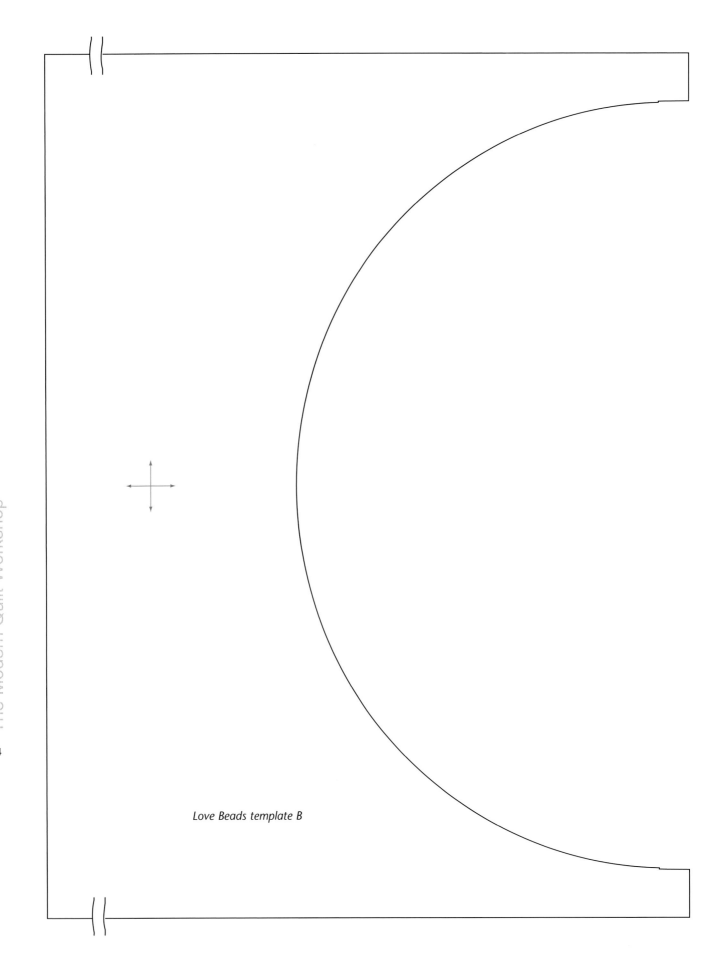

Love Beads template B

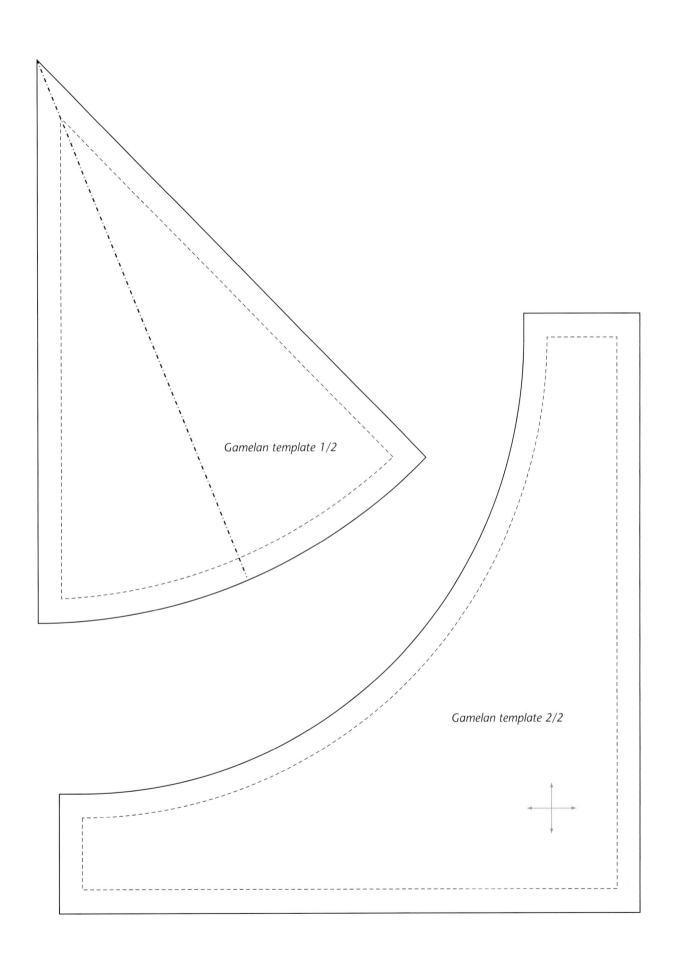

Gamelan template 1/2

Gamelan template 2/2

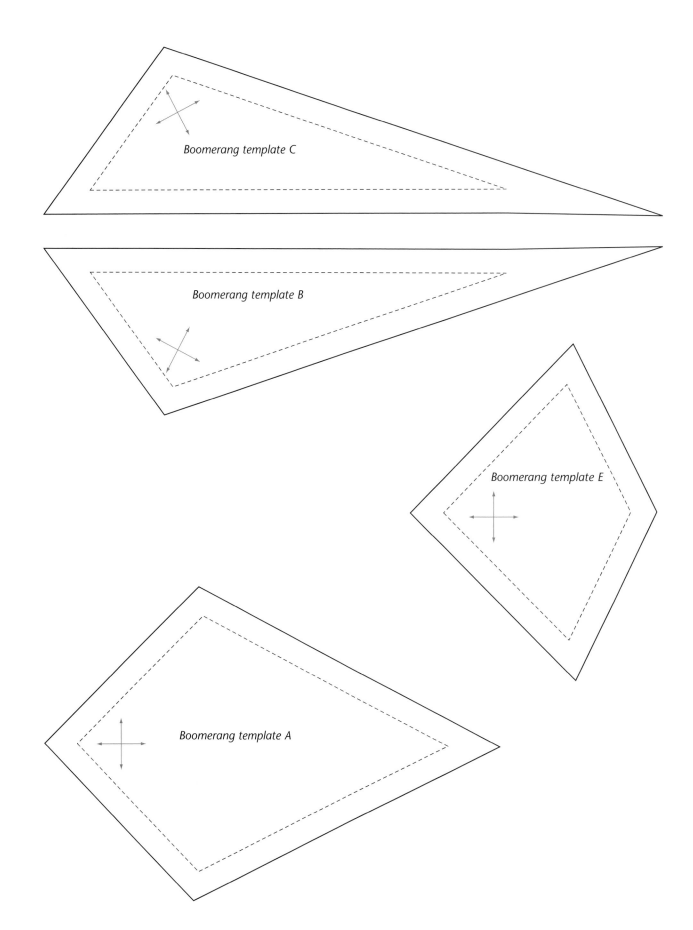

Boomerang template C

Boomerang template B

Boomerang template E

Boomerang template A

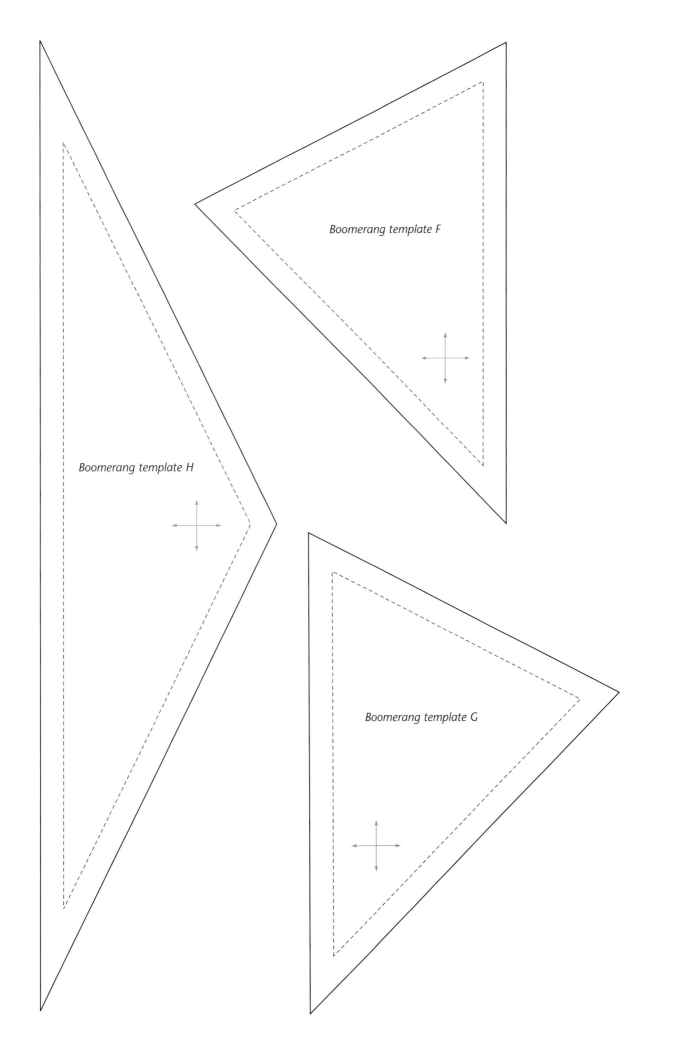

Boomerang template F

Boomerang template H

Boomerang template G

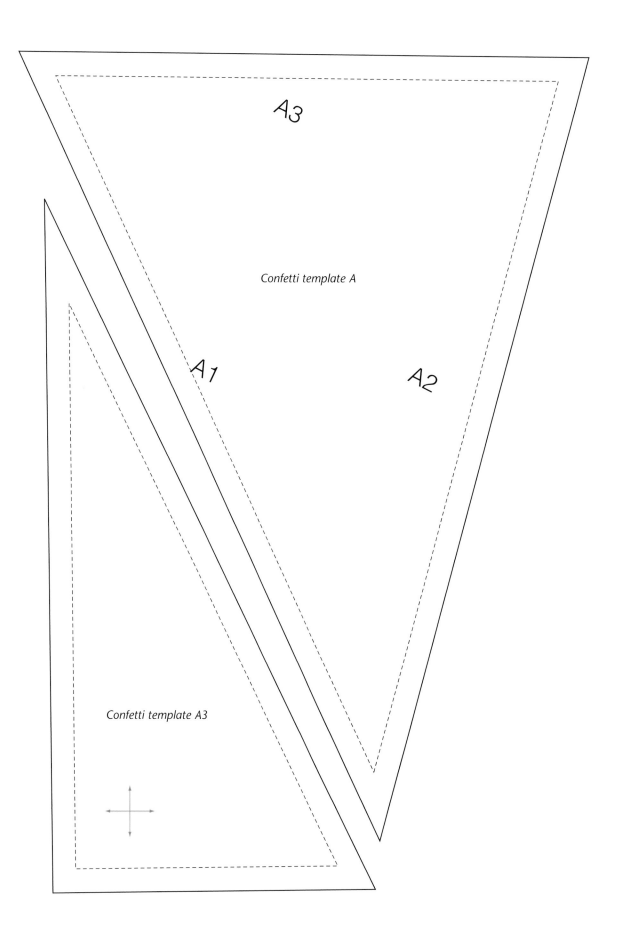

A3

Confetti template A

A1

A2

Confetti template A3

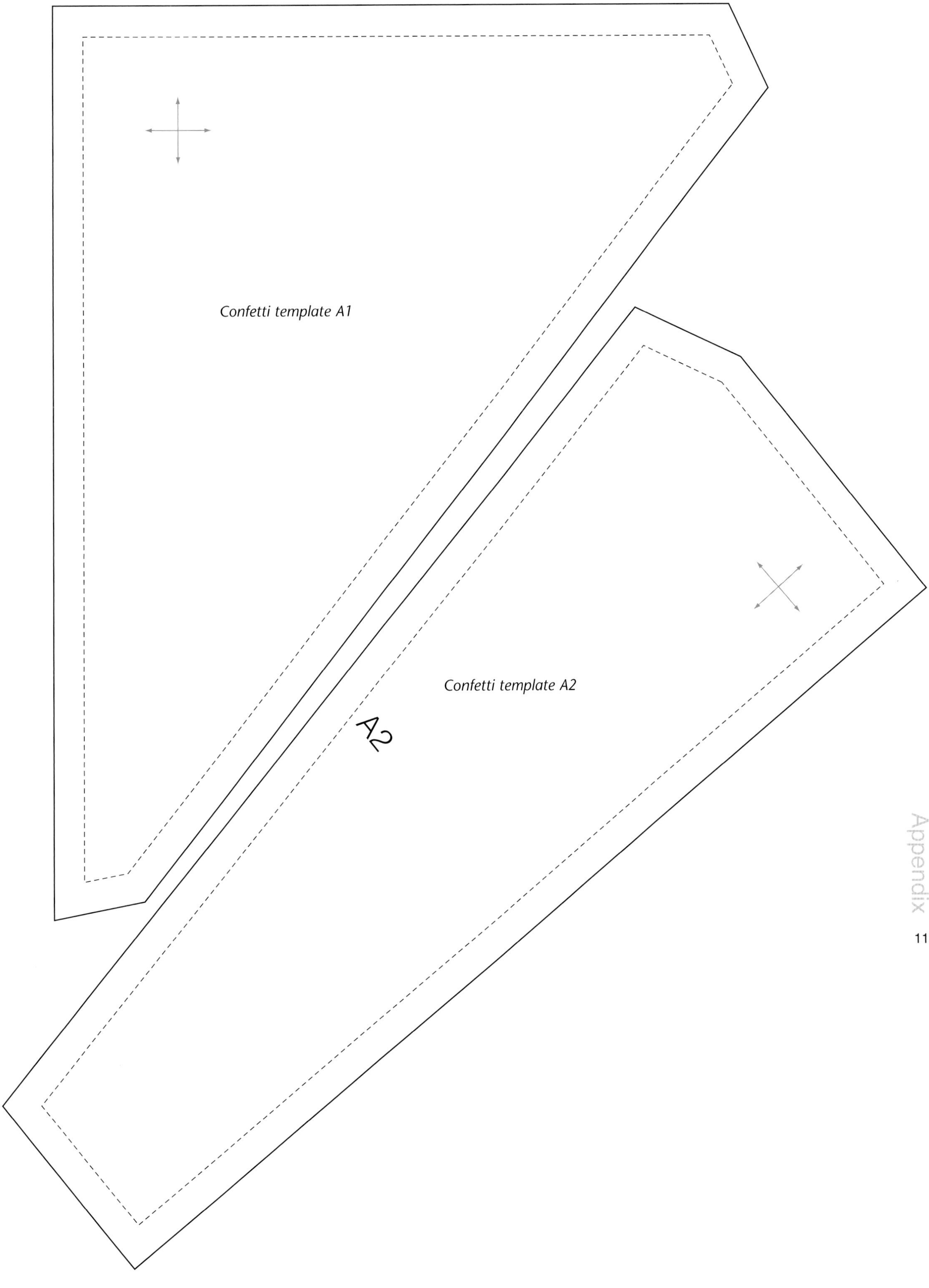

Confetti template A1

Confetti template A2

A2

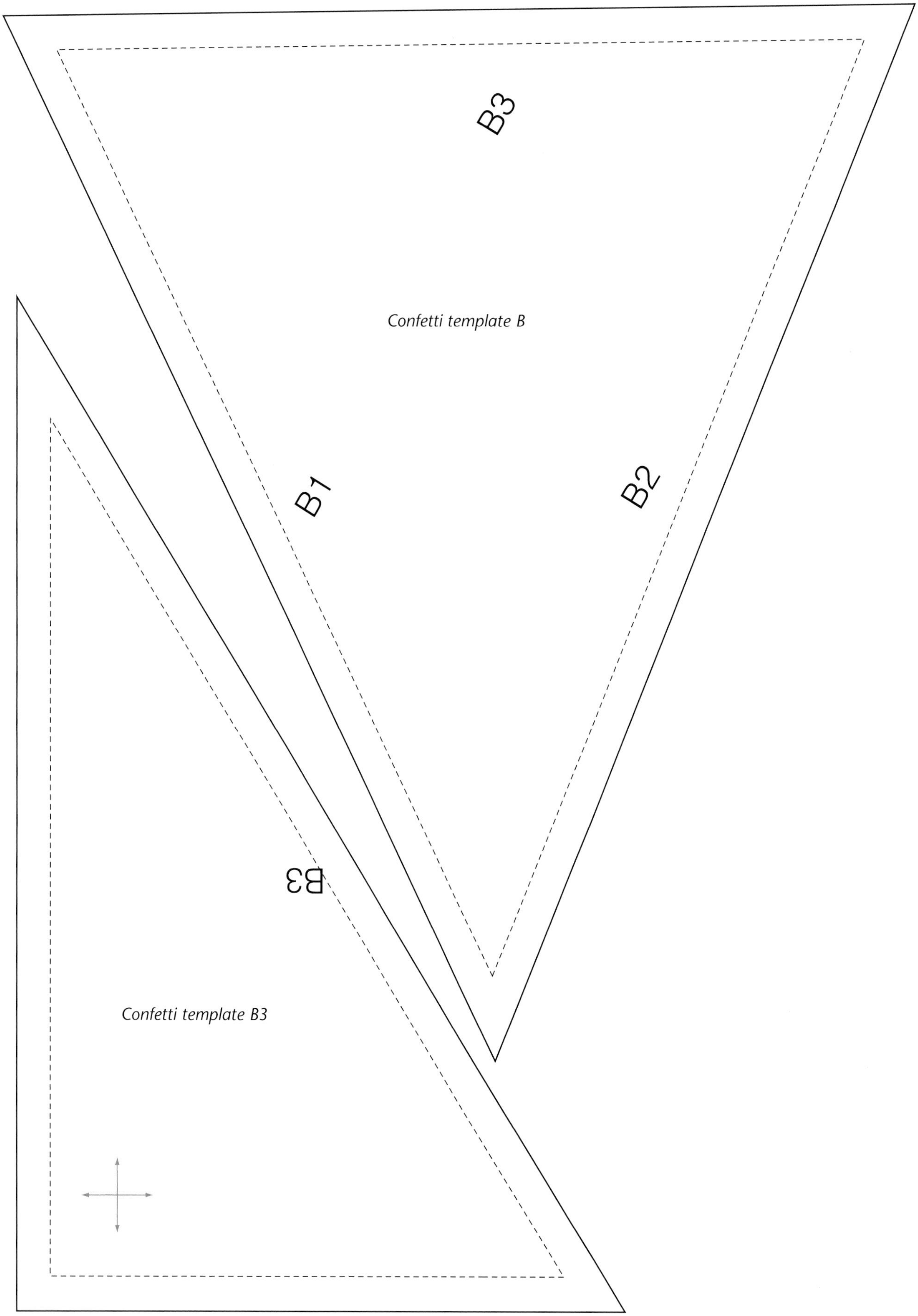

B3

Confetti template B

B1

B2

B3

Confetti template B3

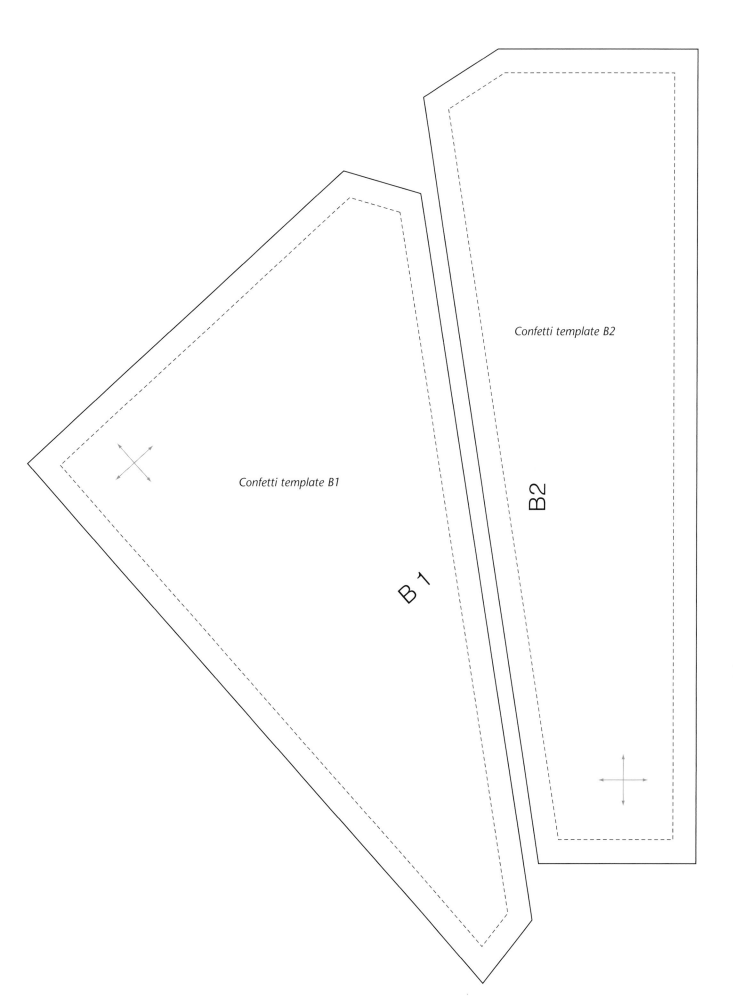

Confetti template B1

Confetti template B2

B1

B2

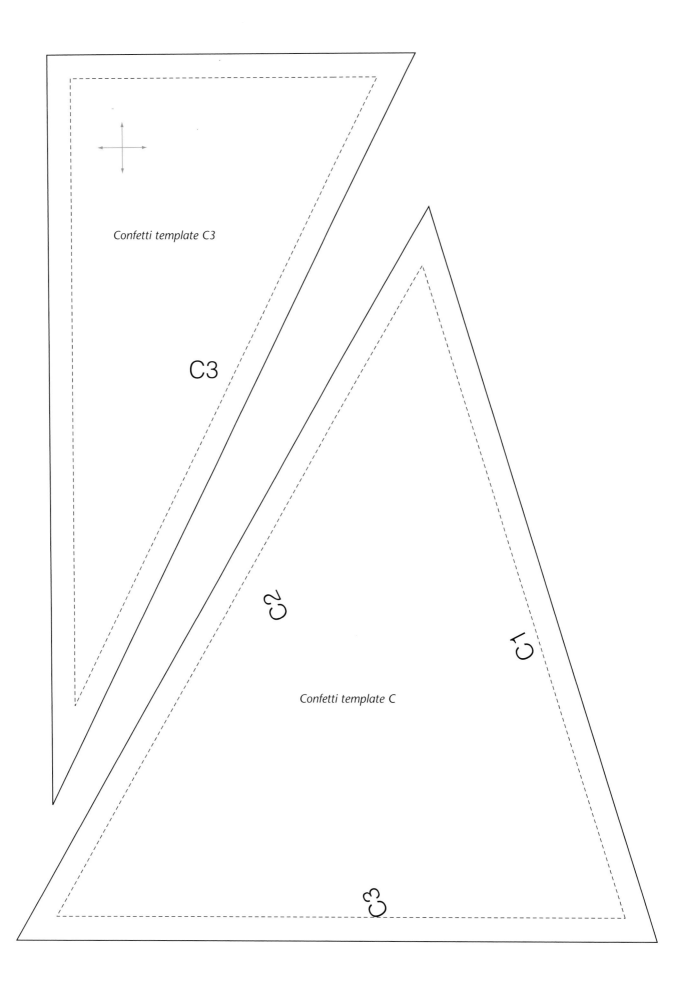

Confetti template C3

C3

C2

C1

Confetti template C

C3

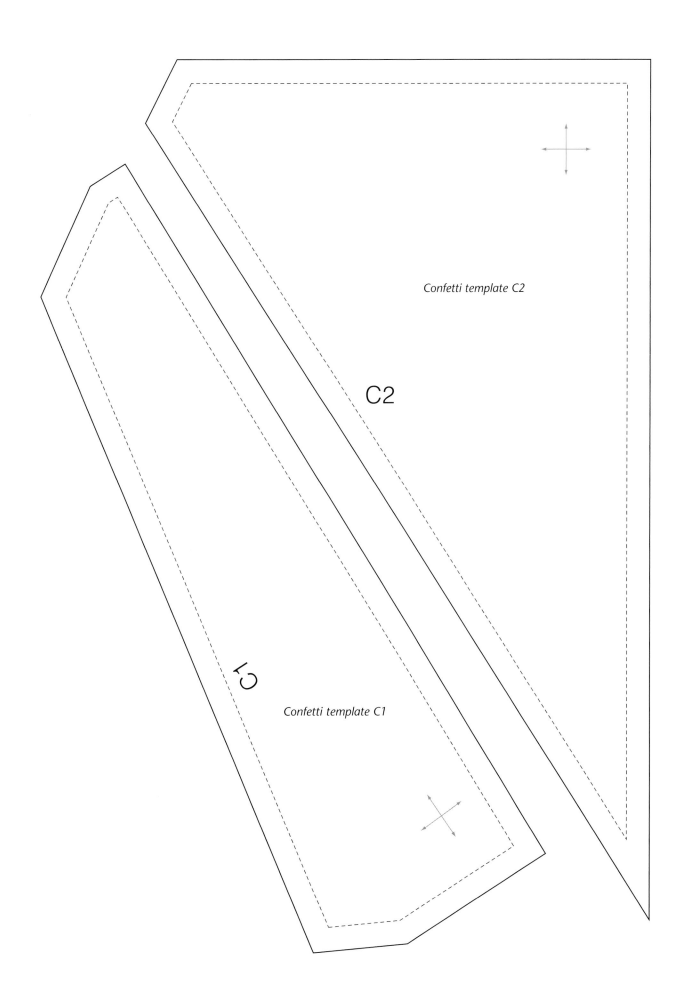

Confetti template C2

C2

C1

Confetti template C1

Resources

The American Folk Art Museum

This museum features the work of primarily self-taught American artists. The museum periodically hosts or curates quilt exhibits and has many important quilts in its permanent collection.

www.folkartmuseum.org
45 W. 53rd Street
New York, NY 10019 USA
212-265-1040

The American Quilter's Society

AQS is famous for its enormous annual quilt show in Paducah, Kentucky, its quilt museum, and its publications.

www.americanquilter.com
P. O. Box 3290
Paducah, KY 42002 USA
270-898-7903 or toll free 800-626-5420

Canadian Quilters' Association/ Association canadienne de la courtepointe

The CQA was formed to promote greater understanding, appreciation, and knowledge of the art, techniques, and heritage of patchwork, appliqué, and quilting; to promote the highest standards of workmanship and design in both traditional and innovative work; and to foster cooperation and sharing among quiltmakers across the country.

www.canadianquilter.com

The Dairy Barn Cultural Arts Center

The Dairy Barn organizes Quilt National, a biennial exhibit of art quilts. It also sponsors a wide range of workshops and classes in quilting and other arts.

www.dairybarn.org
8000 Dairy Lane
Athens, OH 45701 USA
740-592-4981

European Quilt Association

The aim of the European Quilt Association, EQA, is to promote the knowledge of quilting among the member countries: Austria, Belgium, Denmark, Finland, France, Germany, Ireland, Italy, Luxembourg, the Netherlands, Norway, Sweden, Switzerland, and UK.

www.eqa.homepage.dk

International Machine Quilters Association

This site offers many useful links to international and regional machine quilters' resources.

www.imqa.org

The International Quilt Study Center

The University of Nebraska—Lincoln is home to the International Quilt Study Center. It is the only institution that offers a graduate program in textile history and textile design with an emphasis in quilt studies. The IQSC has the country's largest public collection of quilts (more than 1,200) and extensive resources for quilt and textile scholarship. They have a wonderful, searchable database, with images, of their collection.

www.quiltstudy.org
Department of Textiles, Clothing, & Design
University of Nebraska–Lincoln
234 Home Economics Building
Lincoln, NE 68583 USA

The Museum of Arts and Design

Exhibitions of contemporary crafts, including quilts.

www.americancraftmuseum.org
40 W. 53rd Street
New York, NY 10019 USA
212-956-3535

Quilts, Incorporated

Quilts, Inc., is the parent company of Quilt Festival, large consumer shows, and Quilt Market, the largest quilt trade show in America.

www.quilts.com
7660 Woodway, Suite 550
Houston, TX 77063 USA
713-781-6864

The San Jose Museum of Quilts and Textiles

This museum is dedicated to both traditional and contemporary quilts and offers workshops and lectures.

www.sjquiltmuseum.org
110 Paseo de San Antonio
San Jose, CA 95112 USA
408-971-0323

Books

From Fiber to Fabric
Harriet Hargraves

An in-depth book on technical aspects of production and care of quilting textiles.

Available at quilt shops and bookstores everywhere.

The Quilter's Travel Companion

A guidebook, organized by state and region, to more than 2,000 quilting shops across North America. Also includes contact information for hundreds of regional quilting guilds. Available through quilt shops or from:

Chalet Publishing
32 Grand Avenue
Manitou Springs, CO 80829 USA

Quiltmaking by Hand
Jinny Beyer

In-depth instructions on hand quilting.

Available at quilt shops and bookstores everywhere.

Acknowledgments

Truth be told, we had plans to write a different book—one about design. Our students, however, reminded us of the importance of having contemporary patterns available for beginners and people who were not comfortable designing their own quilts. They asked for a book that explained our thinking about quiltmaking and showed our techniques. They knew that this book was not out there and needed to be. They were right, and we thank them for sharing their insights and needs with us.

Our students continue to amaze and inspire us with their enthusiasm and energy. Working with these creative people from around the country is a joy for us. We hope that this book inspires you as much as you have motivated us. Thank you for your constructive criticism of our work and our teaching methods.

For their help in cutting and piecing samples, we are indebted to our two apprentices, Mary

Phemister and Kavita Chaudhary. Their enthusiasm, devotion to craftsmanship, feedback, and attention to detail were invaluable in the development of designs as well as the quilts you see in this book.

We both have been blessed with excellent design educations and thank those who patiently taught us about design, color, and composition. We also thank them for their dedication to teaching and inspiring us to teach others.

Thanks to Mary Ann Hall and Winnie Prentiss of Rockport Publishers for their willingness to learn about the quilting world and their commitment to excellence in publishing.

Finally, we wish to thank our sweet daughter, Sophie, whose cheerfulness and indomitable spirit reminds us daily of what is really important.